THE ULTIMATE DOLLAR COLLAPSE SURVIVAL GUIDE

PROTECT YOUR WEALTH & STOCKPILE LIFE-SAVING SUPPLIES, KEEP YOUR LOVED ONES SAFE IN TIMES OF CRISIS — GET READY BEFORE THE APOCALYPSE

DON CLARK JR.

Copyright © 2025 by Don Clark Jr.

All rights reserved.

No part of this book may be reproduced in any form or by any electronic or mechanical means, including information storage and retrieval systems, without written permission from the author, except for the use of brief quotations in a book review.

INTRODUCTION

The dollar has been called "the safest currency in the world" for decades. It's the backbone of global trade, the symbol of American strength, and the paycheck millions of families rely on. But here's the truth most people don't want to face: **nothing this big lasts forever.**

Every empire has experienced a currency crisis. Rome's silver denarius was debased until it was worthless. In Weimar Germany, a wheelbarrow full of cash couldn't buy a loaf of bread. In Venezuela, people used banknotes as wallpaper. The United States is not immune, and the warning signs are already flashing:

- Rising inflation that erodes your savings.

- Debt levels that can never realistically be repaid.

- Banks and markets wobbling under pressure.

- Supply chains breaking faster than they can be fixed.

You don't have to be an economist to feel it — groceries cost more every month, rent eats a bigger chunk of income, and many Americans are just one crisis away from falling behind.

This book is not about panic. It's about **preparedness.**

When the dollar weakens, when systems fail, when prices explode, your family's survival will depend on the steps you take *before* the headlines turn into chaos.

Inside *The Ultimate Dollar Collapse Survival Guide*, you'll find:

• A **step-by-step 30-day plan** to protect your finances and stockpile essentials.

• Practical checklists for food, water, power, and security.

• Strategies to keep communication open and your family safe when the grid goes dark.

• Simple tools anyone can use — no bunker, no million-dollar budget required.

Preparedness isn't about fear — it's about **freedom.**

Freedom from relying on broken systems. Freedom from worrying if your kids will eat. Freedom from being caught off guard when the world shifts overnight.

By the time you finish this book, you won't just understand what a dollar collapse means. You'll have a plan in motion, confidence in your readiness, and the peace of mind that comes with knowing your loved ones are safe.

The collapse may come slowly. Or it may come all at once. The only thing certain is that when it happens, it will be too late to start preparing.

Let's get ready — step by step, day by day.

PART I — UNDERSTANDING THE COMING COLLAPSE

For most people, the idea of the U.S. dollar collapsing sounds impossible — almost unthinkable. After all, the dollar has been the world's reserve currency for nearly a century. It's the foundation of global trade, the currency most nations still trust, and the money you get paid in, save in, and spend every single day.

But here's the reality: **currencies are not permanent.**

Every empire in history has believed its money was too strong to fail — until it did. Rome debased its coins with cheaper metals until they were worthless. Weimar Germany printed so much cash that wages were carried home in baskets. In Argentina, entire generations watched their savings vanish overnight.

The signs of stress are all around us. Inflation is eating into paychecks faster than raises can keep up. National debt has exploded beyond what can realistically ever be repaid. Banks are wobbling under hidden risks, and supply chains — the lifeblood of everyday life — remain fragile and unstable.

This section of the book is designed to do two things:

1 Strip away the illusions and explain what a dollar collapse would actually look like in your daily life.

2 Show you the early warning signs so you can recognize trouble before it hits the headlines.

Understanding the problem is the first step toward building a solution. If you know what to watch for, you'll never be blindsided. If you understand how fragile the system really is, you'll appreciate why preparation isn't paranoia — it's common sense.

By the end of Part I, you will have a clear picture of:

- What a currency collapse really means (and what it doesn't).

- The red flags that indicate the system is in trouble.

- How to map out your personal risks so you know exactly where to start preparing.

The collapse may not happen tomorrow. It may not even happen this year. But the forces driving it are already in motion, and ignoring them won't make them go away.

The good news? Once you see the danger clearly, you can take smart, practical steps to protect yourself and your family. That's what the rest of this book is all about — but it starts here, with understanding.

1 / WHAT A DOLLAR COLLAPSE REALLY MEANS

When most people hear the phrase *"dollar collapse,"* they imagine something straight out of a Hollywood movie: banks locking their doors overnight, grocery stores stripped bare, riots breaking out in the streets, and the dollar instantly becoming worthless.

While that makes for gripping entertainment, the reality of a currency collapse is usually less dramatic in the moment — but far more dangerous in the long run.

A collapse is rarely one big "bang." It's a process. It begins quietly, with cracks in the system, and grows until trust in the currency is broken. For the average family, this shows up in painfully simple ways: rising prices, shrinking savings, and daily life becoming harder with every passing month.

To prepare, you need to understand what a collapse actually means — not in economic theory, but in **real, everyday consequences**.

THE BASICS: INFLATION, HYPERINFLATION, AND CURRENCY CRISES

Inflation: The Slow Erosion

Inflation is when prices rise over time. A little inflation is normal — it's why your parents could buy a burger for 50 cents, while today the same burger costs $5. But when inflation gets out of control, every dollar you earn buys less and less.

- If inflation runs at 8% a year, $100 today buys only $92 worth of goods a year from now.

- Over 10 years, that same $100 could lose nearly half its purchasing power.

For most people, inflation feels like:

- Groceries costing more each month.

- Gas prices creeping higher.

- Rent taking a bigger share of your paycheck.

Hyperinflation: The Freefall

Hyperinflation is inflation gone wild. Instead of prices rising gradually, they soar by hundreds or thousands of percent in a matter of months — sometimes even weeks.

- In **Weimar Germany (1920s)**, workers carried pay home in wheelbarrows, only to find that a loaf of bread cost billions of marks.

- In **Venezuela (2010s)**, stacks of banknotes became so worthless that people used them as wallpaper or fuel.

Hyperinflation doesn't just hurt savings. It destroys **confidence** in the currency itself. People stop trusting money, turning instead to bartering, foreign cash, or precious metals.

Currency Crises: When Trust Breaks

A currency crisis happens when investors, businesses, or even citizens lose faith in their national money. They rush to dump it for something more stable. The value plunges, and governments scramble to contain the fallout.

- Banks may freeze withdrawals.
- Governments may seize or convert savings accounts.
- Trade slows because no one wants to be paid in a sinking currency.

This is the tipping point — when "normal" life ends, and a survival economy begins.

LESSONS FROM HISTORY

Every empire has thought its money was too strong to fail. Every empire has been wrong.

- **Rome:** The silver denarius was gradually "debased" with cheaper metals until it became almost worthless.
- **Weimar Germany:** Hyperinflation turned salaries into confetti.
- **Argentina:** Savings accounts were frozen and converted into devalued pesos, wiping out decades of hard work.
- **Venezuela:** Salaries collapsed so badly that families used currency for crafts, not purchases.

The United States is not immune. The same pressures — debt, political dysfunction, inflation, loss of trust — are visible today.

WHAT IT WOULD LOOK LIKE IN AMERICA

A U.S. dollar collapse wouldn't necessarily happen in a single day. More likely, it would unfold step by step, hitting families where it hurts most: in their jobs, their savings, and their daily lives.

Jobs

- Businesses cut back as costs rise and imports become more expensive.

- Layoffs increase.

- Companies dependent on global trade or raw materials close their doors.

Savings

- Retirement accounts shrink as markets tumble.

- Cash savings lose value with every month of rising inflation.

- Banks may restrict access, citing "liquidity management."

Daily Life

- Groceries double or triple in price. Shelves thin out as supply chains fail.

- Gas prices spike, making commuting unaffordable.

- Families turn to side hustles, barter, and odd jobs just to keep food on the table.

- Crime and unrest increase as scarcity spreads.

In other words, a collapse isn't abstract. It's not about Wall Street or Washington. It's about **Main Street.** It's about your kitchen, your gas tank, your bank account.

THE MYTH VS. THE REALITY

- **The Myth:** A collapse is a single, overnight disaster.

- **The Reality:** It's a grinding process that eats away at stability until everyday life feels impossible.

That's why so many people get caught off guard — they expect an instant shockwave, when in fact it's more like quicksand pulling them under.

Why This Matters to You

If you're reading this, you've already sensed the warning signs.

- Groceries climbing every month.
- Rent swallowing more of your income.
- News about bank failures, trillion-dollar debts, and government bailouts.

This isn't just politics or headlines. It's your life. A dollar collapse would touch everything you depend on: your job, your savings, your bills, your children's future.

The purpose of this book is not to scare you — it's to **prepare you.**

Once you understand what a collapse really means, you can take smart, practical steps:

- Protect your money.
- Stockpile what you need.
- Build the resilience your family deserves.

A dollar collapse is not just about economics. It's about **survival.**

It means higher prices, harder choices, and more stress in your everyday life. But it also means opportunity: if you see it coming and prepare, you can protect your family while others are caught off guard.

The storm may come slowly. Or it may come suddenly. Either way, once it hits, it will be too late to start preparing.

That's why we begin here, with the truth: **what a dollar collapse really means — for your job, your savings, and your daily life.**

2 / RED FLAGS TO WATCH FOR

Most financial crises do not arrive without warning. The signs are always there — banks under stress, governments overreaching, markets flashing red. The problem is that most people don't recognize the signals until it's too late.

If you want to be ready for a dollar collapse, you need to know **what to watch, where to look, and how to interpret it.**

1. SIGNS FROM BANKS

Banks are supposed to be the backbone of the financial system. But when they start showing cracks, it's often one of the earliest indicators of deeper trouble.

Red flags include:

- **Withdrawal limits or "temporary" restrictions** at ATMs.

- **Bank runs** — long lines of people trying to pull out cash.

- **Regional bank failures** spreading beyond one institution.

- **Mergers or forced bailouts** — when a large bank "absorbs" a failing one.

- **Frozen accounts** or delayed transfers.

If you see any of these happening regularly, it's time to assume that trust in the system is weakening.

2. SIGNS FROM GOVERNMENTS

When governments feel a currency crisis brewing, they scramble to control the narrative. Watch for moves like:

- **Printing more money** (stimulus, bailouts, subsidies) without a real funding source.

- **Price controls** on food, fuel, or rent — which usually lead to shortages.

- **Capital controls,** limiting how much money you can send abroad or exchange.

- **New taxes or "emergency measures"** targeting savings, retirement accounts, or bank deposits.

- **Debt ceilings constantly raised** without credible plans to reduce deficits.

Every one of these steps signals that leaders are fighting to patch a leaking ship with duct tape.

3. SIGNS FROM MARKETS

Markets often reveal cracks before the average person feels them at the grocery store.

Key indicators include:

- **Bond yields spiking** — the government must pay higher interest just to borrow.

- **Stock market volatility** — sharp swings driven by fear and uncertainty.

- **Currency exchange rates** dropping rapidly against other major currencies.

- **Gold and silver prices rising** — investors rushing to safety.

- **Credit rating downgrades** of the nation's debt.

These are the "canaries in the coal mine" of the global economy. When investors run for cover, it's only a matter of time before ordinary citizens feel the shock.

4. HISTORICAL CASE STUDIES

To see how these red flags play out, we only have to look at history.

Weimar Germany (1920s)

- Government printed money to pay off war debts.

- Inflation exploded → workers demanded wages twice a day.

- Families burned banknotes for heat because they were cheaper than firewood.

- The key warning sign: **money supply ballooned with no backing.**

Argentina (2001, 2018, 2023)

- Savings accounts were **frozen** and forcibly converted into weaker pesos.

- Middle-class families lost decades of savings.

- Imports vanished, unemployment soared.

- The key warning sign: **capital controls and frozen bank accounts.**

Venezuela (2010s)

- Hyperinflation made salaries worthless within weeks.

- People abandoned their currency, bartering for food and medicine.

- Government kept printing more, making the crisis spiral.

- The key warning sign: **runaway inflation with no trust in leadership.**

Each case is different, but the pattern is the same: governments print more, banks weaken, markets panic, and ordinary people are left holding worthless money.

5. YOUR RED FLAG CHECKLIST

Keep this simple list handy and update it regularly. If you start seeing multiple boxes checked, the storm is closer than you think:

✓ Banks limiting withdrawals or freezing accounts

✓ Regional bank failures spreading nationwide

✓ Government printing money without control

✓ Price controls or emergency taxes on savings

✓ Capital controls or limits on currency exchange

✓ Bond yields spiking, dollar weakening against other currencies

✓ Gold/silver prices surging fast

✓ Savings accounts losing value due to inflation

✓ Rising unrest, protests, or shortages

A dollar collapse will not arrive without warning. The signs will be everywhere — in your bank, in government policies, in financial markets, and in the news. History has shown us the script again and again.

The only question is whether you'll recognize those signals in time to act.

3 / YOUR PERSONAL RISK MAP

PREPAREDNESS BEGINS WITH AWARENESS. Before you can build a solid plan, you need to know **where you stand today**. Every family has different strengths and weaknesses, and recognizing them early is what separates those who thrive from those who struggle when crisis strikes.

This chapter will help you create a **Personal Risk Map** — a clear picture of your vulnerabilities in four key areas: **financial, food, energy, and security**.

STEP 1: THE SELF-ASSESSMENT EXERCISE

Take a notebook or print this section. Answer honestly. The goal is not perfection but clarity.

A. Financial Preparedness

- Do you have at least **one month of expenses** in cash or savings?
- Are your savings spread across more than one bank or institution?
- Do you keep some **cash at home** for emergencies?
- Do you own any inflation-resistant assets (gold, silver, real goods)?

- Do you have copies of important documents stored safely?

Score yourself:

- 4–5 "Yes" answers = Strong
- 2–3 "Yes" answers = Moderate
- 0–1 "Yes" answers = Vulnerable

B. Food Preparedness

- Do you keep at least **two weeks of shelf-stable food** at home?
- Could you cook meals if the power went out (camp stove, propane, solar oven)?
- Do you know how to rotate pantry items to avoid waste?
- Do you store extra cooking essentials (oil, salt, spices)?
- Do you have a garden, livestock, or access to local food sources?

Score yourself:

- 4–5 "Yes" answers = Strong
- 2–3 "Yes" answers = Moderate
- 0–1 "Yes" answers = Vulnerable

C. Energy Preparedness

- Do you have a backup power source (generator, solar, battery bank)?
- Do you keep spare fuel safely stored?
- Do you own alternative light sources (lanterns, candles, solar lamps)?

- Could you heat at least one room in your home without the grid?
- Do you know how to safely use and maintain your energy backups?

Score yourself:

- 4–5 "Yes" answers = Strong
- 2–3 "Yes" answers = Moderate
- 0–1 "Yes" answers = Vulnerable

D. Security Preparedness

- Do you have secure locks, reinforced doors, or an alarm system?
- Do you know your neighbors and have a basic community support network?
- Do you have a plan for family communication during an emergency?
- Do you keep self-defense tools (firearms, pepper spray, non-lethal options) and know how to use them safely?
- Do you practice situational awareness when outside your home?

Score yourself:

- 4–5 "Yes" answers = Strong
- 2–3 "Yes" answers = Moderate
- 0–1 "Yes" answers = Vulnerable

STEP 2: IDENTIFY WHICH VULNERABILITIES MATTER MOST

After scoring each category, you now have a clear picture of your current resilience.

- If your **Financial** score is weak → inflation, job loss, or banking restrictions will hit you hardest.

- If your **Food** score is weak → even minor supply chain issues could leave your family hungry.

- If your **Energy** score is weak → power outages will make survival difficult, especially in extreme heat or cold.

- If your **Security** score is weak → shortages and unrest will make your household a target.

Your lowest score is where you should start.

STEP 3: BUILD YOUR PERSONAL RISK MAP

Draw a simple square divided into four sections: **Financial, Food, Energy, Security.**

- Shade each section based on your score (Strong = green, Moderate = yellow, Vulnerable = red).

- This becomes your **Risk Map** — a visual guide to where you need to focus first.

Preparedness is not about doing everything at once. It's about **knowing your weak points and strengthening them step by step.**

By completing this exercise, you now have a personal roadmap. You know whether to begin with your finances, your pantry, your power supply, or your security. In the next chapters, we'll dig deeper into each of these areas and give you the tools to turn every "Vulnerable" into "Strong."

PART II — PROTECTING YOUR MONEY

When a currency weakens, the first place most people feel it is in their wallet. Rising prices, shrinking savings, and unstable banks can erase years of hard work in a matter of months. The truth is simple: **if you don't take steps to defend your money, no one else will.**

This section is about building a **financial shield** strong enough to weather a dollar collapse. You don't need to be an economist or a Wall Street insider. What you need is clarity, smart strategies, and tools that ordinary families can actually use.

In the chapters ahead, we'll cover:

- How to **protect cash** and reduce your exposure to bank failures.

- Which government-backed assets can guard against inflation.

- How to buy and store **gold and silver** without falling for scams.

- The simple but powerful **Emergency Financial Folder** that keeps your family prepared to act quickly in any crisis.

Your job, your savings, your retirement, and your daily stability are all tied to the dollar. If that dollar collapses, the systems you rely on will shake — but with the right plan, you don't have to go down with them.

By the end of this section, you'll know exactly how to safeguard your money, defend what you've earned, and stay one step ahead of the chaos.

4 / CASH & BANK SAFETY

When a dollar collapse looms, the first place most families look for stability is their bank account. After all, we've been taught from childhood that banks are safe, regulated, and insured. But history and recent headlines tell a different story: banks are only as strong as the system behind them, and when that system is under stress, **your money can be locked, limited, or even lost.**

This chapter will give you the tools to protect your cash, structure your accounts wisely, and keep a safe reserve at home — so you're not caught empty-handed when it matters most.

FDIC INSURANCE: WHAT IT REALLY MEANS

Most Americans believe that as long as their deposits are "FDIC insured," they are fully protected. The truth is more complicated.

- **FDIC coverage is capped at $250,000 per depositor, per bank, per account type.**
  - If you and your spouse each hold an account, that doubles the coverage.

- If you spread accounts across multiple banks, each is insured separately.

- **Coverage applies only if the bank fails.** It does not protect against:

- Inflation reducing your money's value.

- Frozen accounts during a crisis.

- Delayed access when banks impose withdrawal limits.

- **Payouts are not instant.** Even when the FDIC covers a failed bank, it can take days or weeks before you regain access. In a fast-moving collapse, that delay can be devastating.

Bottom line: FDIC protection is helpful but limited. It's not a magic shield against a currency crisis.

SMART ACCOUNT STRUCTURES

Instead of leaving all your money in one place, think like a prepper: **diversify your financial storage.**

1 Multiple Banks

- Spread accounts across different institutions (local, regional, national, and even credit unions).

- If one freezes or fails, you're not locked out completely.

2 Account Types

- Keep a mix of checking, savings, and possibly money market accounts.

- Different structures may have different withdrawal rules and protections.

3 Joint vs. Individual Accounts

- Remember that FDIC insurance applies **per depositor.**

○ Example: A joint account with your spouse covers $500,000 instead of $250,000.

4 Credit Union Advantage

○ Credit unions are insured by the NCUA, with the same $250,000 limit.

○ They are often more community-based and less exposed to risky trading.

5 Liquidity First

○ Keep enough in easily accessible accounts to cover **at least 1–2 months of expenses.**

○ Avoid tying up too much in accounts with penalties or delays.

Think of it like building compartments on a ship: if one floods, the whole vessel doesn't sink.

CASH AT HOME: YOUR EMERGENCY RESERVE

In a collapse, electronic banking may fail or freeze. That's why every prepared household needs a **cash reserve at home.**

How Much?

• Aim for **at least two weeks of essential expenses** in physical cash.

• More if you live in a high-cost area or depend heavily on electronic payments.

Denominations Matter

• Small bills ($1s, $5s, $10s, $20s) are more useful than large notes.

• In a crisis, few people will want to break a $100.

Storage Tips

• Avoid obvious places like sock drawers or under mattresses.

- Use a **fireproof, waterproof safe** bolted to the floor or hidden in a wall.

- Spread small amounts in multiple locations inside your home.

Safety First

- Don't announce your cash reserve to friends or neighbors.

- Keep it discreet, secure, and only known to trusted family members.

A THREE-TIER CASH STRATEGY

1 **Bank Accounts (Main Operating Funds):** Paychecks, bills, and normal spending.

2 **Diversified Accounts (Protected Savings):** Spread across banks, structured for insurance and redundancy.

3 **Home Cash Reserve (Emergency Liquidity):** Small bills, secure storage, ready for immediate use.

This layered system means you can function in normal times, weather a bank failure, and still operate if the grid or banking system goes down.

Relying on a single bank account is like keeping all your survival gear in one backpack and leaving it by the front door — one failure, and you're stranded. By diversifying your accounts, knowing FDIC limits, and holding a secure cash reserve at home, you build resilience against the first wave of a dollar collapse.

When the headlines hit and others line up outside ATMs, you'll already have what you need.

5 / TREASURIES & INFLATION HEDGES

INFLATION IS OFTEN CALLED the "silent thief." Unlike a stock market crash or a sudden bank failure, inflation works quietly, day after day, stealing the value of your savings without you even noticing. One morning you realize your paycheck buys less food, your rent takes up more of your income, and the "safe" cash sitting in the bank is shrinking in real terms.

The good news? There are tools available to ordinary Americans that can help hedge against inflation and provide a buffer in uncertain times. They're not glamorous, and they won't make you rich overnight — but they can protect what you already have.

UNDERSTANDING TREASURIES

U.S. Treasuries are debt securities issued by the federal government. In plain English, you're lending money to the U.S. government in exchange for guaranteed interest payments.

Types include:

- **Treasury Bills (T-Bills):** Mature in less than a year.
- **Treasury Notes (T-Notes):** Mature in 2–10 years.

- **Treasury Bonds (T-Bonds):** Mature in 20–30 years.

Why they matter in a collapse scenario:

- They are considered one of the **safest investments** in the world because they're backed by the U.S. government.

- If banks wobble, Treasuries remain a direct claim on the government — not a private institution.

- They can be bought directly from TreasuryDirect.gov with no middleman.

TIPS: TREASURY INFLATION-PROTECTED SECURITIES

TIPS are a special kind of Treasury bond designed specifically to fight inflation.

- **How they work:** The principal value of your bond rises with inflation (measured by the Consumer Price Index). When prices rise, your investment adjusts upward.

- **Payout:** You earn interest on this adjusted amount, so both your interest payments and the final payout keep pace with inflation.

- **When they help most:** Periods of rising prices when cash in the bank is losing purchasing power.

Example:

- You invest $1,000 in TIPS. Inflation runs at 8% for the year.

- Your principal is adjusted to $1,080.

- Your interest is then calculated on $1,080, not $1,000.

This doesn't make you wealthy — but it prevents you from quietly being robbed by inflation.

I BONDS: A TOOL FOR EVERYDAY SAVERS

Series I Savings Bonds (I Bonds) are another U.S. government tool to protect against inflation.

- **Fixed + Variable Rate:** Part of your return is fixed, while the other part adjusts every six months with inflation.

- **Low Risk:** Like TIPS, they're backed by the government.

- **Limit:** You can buy up to $10,000 per year per person (plus $5,000 more if you use your tax refund).

- **Access:** Must be purchased through TreasuryDirect.gov.

Why they're powerful:

- They allow ordinary families to park money safely while inflation is high.

- They're simple, with no complicated market moves.

LADDERING: BUILDING FLEXIBILITY

One smart strategy is **laddering Treasuries.**

- Instead of locking up all your money in one bond, you spread it across multiple maturities (3 months, 1 year, 2 years, 5 years, etc.).

- As each matures, you can reinvest or use the cash.

- This creates both **flexibility** and **stability.**

Think of it as a staggered emergency fund that keeps refreshing itself.

PROS AND CONS

Pros:

- Backed by the U.S. government (one of the safest options).

- Direct hedge against inflation (TIPS, I Bonds).

- Accessible to ordinary savers via TreasuryDirect.

- Not tied to the banking system.

Cons:

- Limited growth (won't make you rich).

- Purchase limits (I Bonds cap at $10,000/year).

- Locked funds for a set period (some penalties if withdrawn early).

- Government-controlled (in extreme collapse, access could still be restricted).

You don't have to be a Wall Street investor to protect yourself from inflation. By using simple tools like TIPS, I Bonds, and a Treasury ladder, you can keep your savings from evaporating while others watch their cash lose value.

In uncertain times, wealth is not about chasing big gains. It's about **protecting purchasing power** so your family can still afford food, fuel, and shelter when prices soar.

6 / GOLD & SILVER WITHOUT THE HYPE

Whenever financial chaos makes the news, you'll hear people shouting: *"Buy gold! Buy silver!"* The metals market is full of hype, fear, and aggressive sales tactics. The truth is simpler: **gold and silver are tools — not magic.**

Used wisely, they can protect your purchasing power and give you confidence when paper money falters. Used foolishly, they can drain your savings or leave you with assets you can't use.

This chapter strips away the hype and gives you a clear, practical plan for adding precious metals to your survival toolkit.

WHY PRECIOUS METALS MATTER

Gold and silver have been trusted for thousands of years. Unlike paper money, they can't be printed at will. Unlike stocks, they don't depend on corporate profits.

- **Gold** is a store of wealth. It holds value over centuries and is best for preserving large amounts of purchasing power.

- **Silver** is both money and a practical metal. It's more affordable, easier to trade in small amounts, and often in higher demand during crises.

In short: gold = stability, silver = flexibility.

FORMS OF GOLD AND SILVER TO BUY

1 Coins (Best for Beginners & Barter)

- **Gold Eagles, Krugerrands, Canadian Maple Leafs** (1 oz).
- **Silver Eagles, Silver Maple Leafs, generic rounds** (1 oz).
- Easy to recognize, hard to counterfeit, highly liquid.
- Best for: small trades, everyday preparedness.

2 Bars & Bullion (Best for Long-Term Storage)

- Gold bars (1 oz, 10 oz, 1 kg).
- Silver bars (10 oz, 100 oz).
- Lower premiums over spot price compared to coins.
- Best for: storing larger sums safely, not for daily barter.

3 Junk Silver (Hidden Gem)

- Pre-1965 U.S. dimes, quarters, and half-dollars contain 90% silver.
- Small denominations = excellent for barter.
- Often sold in bags by face value (e.g., $100 face).

4 ETFs and Digital Gold (Caution)

- Paper gold (like GLD ETFs) tracks the price but doesn't give you physical ownership.
- Convenient for investing, but useless if the financial system seizes up.
- Best for: diversification in a regular portfolio, not survival prepping.

STORAGE: KEEP IT SAFE, KEEP IT SMART

- **At Home:**

  ○ Fireproof safe, hidden location, don't advertise.

  ○ Store silver for barter and some small gold for emergencies.

- **Professional Storage:**

  ○ Bank safe deposit box (risk: locked out during crisis).

  ○ Private vault services (safer but with fees).

- **Rule of Thumb:**

  ○ Keep enough physical metal at home to cover **1–2 months of basic needs**.

  ○ Store the rest in a secure, long-term facility.

MISTAKES TO AVOID

1 Overpaying Premiums

○ Some dealers push "rare" or "collectible" coins at huge markups.

○ For survival, you want bullion value, not collector's value.

2 All-In Mentality

○ Don't dump all your savings into metals. They protect wealth — they don't produce income.

3 Ignoring Liquidity

○ A 1-kilo gold bar looks impressive, but you can't trade it for groceries. Small denominations are critical.

4 Forgetting Security

○ Owning gold and silver makes you a target if others know.

○ Keep purchases private, storage discreet, and only share with trusted family.

A BALANCED APPROACH

- **Start with silver:** Easy entry point, small trades possible.
- **Add gold gradually:** For preserving larger chunks of savings.
- **Mix coins and bars:** Coins for flexibility, bars for long-term value.
- **Avoid collectibles:** Stick to well-known bullion products.

Gold and silver aren't about getting rich. They're about **not getting wiped out.** In a dollar collapse, they act as your backup currency — wealth you can trust when paper money fails.

Used wisely, they're an anchor of stability in a storm. Used recklessly, they're just another trap.

7 / THE EMERGENCY FINANCIAL FOLDER

WHEN A CRISIS STRIKES, confusion kills time — and time costs money. Families who know where their documents, accounts, and critical information are stored have a major advantage. Families who don't may find themselves locked out of banks, unable to prove ownership, or wasting precious hours searching for papers in the middle of an emergency.

The solution is simple: build an **Emergency Financial Folder (EFF)** — a single, organized binder (or digital backup) that contains everything you and your loved ones need to function financially when the dollar collapses. Think of it as your financial go-bag.

STEP 1: CHOOSE THE RIGHT FORMAT

- **Physical Binder:**

  ○ Fireproof, waterproof folder or safe.

  ○ Organized with dividers (banking, insurance, property, ID, etc.).

- **Digital Backup:**

  ○ Encrypted USB drive or external hard drive.

○ Cloud storage with two-factor authentication (but only if you trust your security).

☞ Best practice: **Do both.** Keep one physical binder in a safe place at home and one encrypted digital copy offsite.

STEP 2: GATHER ESSENTIAL DOCUMENTS

Here's your **checklist of must-have items:**

Personal Identification

- Birth certificates
- Passports
- Social Security cards
- Driver's licenses / state IDs
- Marriage/divorce certificates

Financial Accounts

- Bank account details (account numbers, routing numbers)
- Credit and debit card info (front/back copies)
- Retirement accounts (401k, IRA, pension)
- Investment accounts (brokerage, TreasuryDirect, etc.)

Property & Assets

- Deeds, titles, and mortgage papers
- Vehicle titles, insurance policies
- Precious metal receipts and storage details
- Safe deposit box info and keys

Insurance & Medical

- Health insurance cards and policy numbers
- Life insurance policies
- Homeowner's or renter's insurance policies
- Medical records, prescriptions, and doctor contacts

Emergency Cash

- A small reserve of **physical cash in small bills** ($1, $5, $10, $20).
- Keep inside the binder or in the same safe.

Passwords & Access

- Master list of critical login info (preferably stored in a password manager, with backup recovery codes).
- PINs or account recovery instructions.

Legal Documents

- Wills and powers of attorney
- Living wills/medical directives
- Guardianship or custody papers

STEP 3: KEEP IT CURRENT

An outdated folder is almost as bad as no folder at all.

- Review every **6 months.**
- Update expired IDs, new accounts, new policies.
- Rotate the emergency cash if bills get old or damaged.

STEP 4: SHARE WITH TRUSTED PEOPLE

Your family needs to know this exists.

- Tell your spouse, adult children, or one trusted friend where the folder is stored.
- Leave clear instructions for access (safe combination, key location).
- Never share widely — security matters.

STEP 5: DRILL YOUR BINDER

Preparedness is practice. Once your folder is built, run a family drill:

- Pretend you need to evacuate in 5 minutes.
- Grab the folder.
- See if you can access everything you'd need: cash, IDs, account info.

If it feels clunky, reorganize until it works smoothly.

Your **Emergency Financial Folder** is more than paperwork. It's a shield against chaos. In a collapse, you may lose access to banks, credit cards, or even your home. But with a single grab-and-go binder, you carry proof of who you are, what you own, and how to access your resources.

It's simple, powerful, and absolutely essential.

PART III – SECURING YOUR HOME BASE

Money matters, but when systems fail, survival starts at home. Your house — whether it's a city apartment, a suburban townhouse, or a rural farmhouse — becomes the center of your family's safety. If the dollar weakens, supply chains falter, or the grid goes down, your **home base is your fortress.**

This section gives you the tools to build resilience where it matters most:

- **Food and Water:** Stockpile smart, rotate supplies, and secure clean drinking water.

- **Power and Heat:** Keep the lights on and your family warm, even if the grid goes dark.

- **Medical and Hygiene:** Care for injuries, prevent illness, and maintain morale under stress.

- **Security:** Protect what you've prepared from theft, unrest, or desperation.

You don't need a bunker or an off-grid compound. You need a clear plan, the right supplies, and practical steps that work in everyday homes.

By the end of this part, you'll have a **72-hour kit ready, a two-week pantry plan, clean water secured, backup power in place, and a home that's safer against threats.** In other words: a base strong enough to carry your family through crisis.

8 / THE 72-HOUR SURVIVAL KIT

In every disaster — hurricanes, blackouts, economic collapses — the first 72 hours are the most critical. Government agencies like FEMA recommend that every household be ready to survive on their own for at least three days. Why? Because emergency services are often overwhelmed, supply chains are disrupted, and help can take days to arrive.

That's why building a **72-Hour Survival Kit** is step one for every prepared family. This kit is your lifeline, designed to cover the essentials: food, water, medicine, power, and protection.

WHAT IS A 72-HOUR KIT?

A **72-hour kit** is a pre-packed collection of supplies that sustains you and your family for three full days without outside help. It should be:

- **Portable:** Easy to grab and carry if you need to evacuate.
- **Accessible:** Stored in a location you can reach quickly.
- **Customized:** Tailored to your family's specific needs.

Think of it as a **"survival starter pack"** that buys you time to adapt, relocate, or wait for support.

THE ESSENTIALS

Here's a breakdown of what every kit must contain:

1. Water

- Minimum: **1 gallon per person, per day** (3 gallons per person for 72 hours).
- Options: bottled water, water pouches, or refillable containers.
- Add a small filter or purification tablets in case supplies run out.

2. Food

- 3 days of **non-perishable, ready-to-eat foods.**
- Examples: energy bars, canned meat, canned beans, rice, pasta, peanut butter, trail mix.
- Don't forget utensils (can opener, spork, camping knife).

3. Shelter & Warmth

- Emergency blankets (Mylar space blankets).
- Lightweight sleeping bags or bivvy sacks.
- Ponchos or tarps (for makeshift shelter if displaced).

4. Light & Power

- Flashlights (LED preferred).
- Headlamps (keep hands free).
- Extra batteries.
- Small solar charger or power bank for phones/radios.

5. First Aid & Hygiene

- First aid kit (bandages, antiseptics, gloves, tweezers, gauze).
- Prescription meds (at least 3-day supply).
- Pain relievers, allergy meds.
- Hygiene items: toothbrush, toothpaste, wet wipes, hand sanitizer, soap.

6. Communication

- Battery-powered or hand-crank NOAA weather radio.
- Whistle for signaling.
- Printed contact list (don't rely only on phones).

7. Safety & Tools

- Multipurpose tool (like a Leatherman or Swiss Army knife).
- Matches, lighter, or fire starter.
- Duct tape, paracord, small sewing kit.
- Pepper spray or self-defense tool if legal in your state.

8. Documents & Cash

- Copies of IDs, insurance cards, and bank info (store in waterproof bag).
- Emergency cash in small bills ($1s, $5s, $10s).

CUSTOMIZING FOR YOUR FAMILY

No two households are alike. Your kit must reflect your reality.

- **Families with Children:** Add formula, diapers, small toys, comfort items.
- **Elderly Members:** Extra meds, mobility aids, large-print instructions.

- **Pets:** Food, water, leash, vaccination records, waste bags.

- **Special Needs:** Medical equipment, dietary needs, spare glasses or hearing aid batteries.

Storage & Accessibility

- Keep kits in a **grab-and-go backpack** for each family member.

- Store near an exit (closet by the door, garage shelf).

- If possible, build **two kits**: one for home, one for your vehicle.

PRO TIP: THE "RULE OF THREES"

In survival, remember the Rule of Threes:

- 3 minutes without air.

- 3 hours without shelter (in extreme conditions).

- 3 days without water.

- 3 weeks without food.

Your kit is designed around this rule — keeping you alive through the critical window when chaos is at its peak.

The **72-Hour Kit** is not just about surviving three days. It's about giving you a foundation of confidence, knowing you can handle immediate disruption while others panic. Once you've built this, you can move on to bigger preparations — like the two-week pantry and long-term storage.

9 / THE TWO-WEEK PANTRY PLAN

THE 72-HOUR KIT gets you through the first critical days. But history shows that many crises last longer. Hurricanes, supply chain breakdowns, power grid failures, and currency crashes often stretch into weeks. That's why every prepared household needs a **Two-Week Pantry Plan.**

This isn't about panic-buying or filling your garage with junk food. It's about **building a balanced, practical, and affordable food reserve** that your family will actually eat.

STEP 1: THE FORMULA FOR TWO WEEKS

A good target is:

- **2,000 calories per adult per day** (adjust for children or activity level).
- **3 meals + 1 snack per person per day.**
- **14 days × number of family members.**

  For a family of 4, that's roughly **168 meals + 56 snacks.**

STEP 2: FOOD CATEGORIES THAT WORK

Choose foods that are:

- **Shelf-Stable:** Lasts months or years.
- **Easy to Prepare:** Minimal cooking, water, or power needed.
- **Nutritious:** Not just calories, but protein, fiber, and vitamins.

Pantry Staples

- Rice, pasta, oats, lentils, beans, quinoa.
- Canned meats (chicken, tuna, salmon, spam).
- Canned vegetables and fruit.
- Nut butters, honey, powdered milk.
- Cooking basics: oil, salt, sugar, spices.

Quick-Use Foods

- Protein bars, trail mix, granola.
- Crackers, tortillas, shelf-stable bread.
- Freeze-dried meals (lightweight, long shelf life).

STEP 3: SAMPLE TWO-WEEK MENU

Here's an example rotation you can adapt:

- **Breakfasts:** oatmeal with dried fruit, granola with powdered milk, peanut butter on crackers.
- **Lunches:** canned tuna wraps, lentil soup, rice with beans.
- **Dinners:** pasta with canned tomato sauce, canned chicken stew with rice, chili made from beans and canned beef.
- **Snacks:** trail mix, jerky, dried fruit, nuts.

Rotating these meals gives variety while keeping supplies simple.

STEP 4: STORAGE & ROTATION

Golden Rule: *Store what you eat, eat what you store.*

- Label items with **purchase date** and **expiration date**.
- Use the **FIFO method**: First In, First Out.
- Check your pantry every **3 months** — restock what you've used.

This way, your pantry is always fresh, and nothing goes to waste.

STEP 5: DON'T FORGET THE EXTRAS

Beyond calories, you'll need:

- **Cooking fuel** (propane, butane, charcoal).
- **Can opener** (manual).
- **Comfort foods** (coffee, tea, chocolate, spices).
- **Special needs** (baby formula, gluten-free, medical diets).

STEP 6: TRACKING WITH A PLANNER

A written plan makes everything easier. Create a **14-day chart** with columns for:

- Day | Breakfast | Lunch | Dinner | Snack | Notes

This not only organizes meals but also makes it simple for any family member to know what's next.

👉 (Bonus: You'll have this planner included as a printable PDF to customize.)

. . .

The Two-Week Pantry Plan is about **control.** Instead of worrying if shelves will be empty tomorrow, you'll know your family has food, nutrition, and stability for 14 days. From there, you can scale up to months of preparedness — but two weeks is the foundation that turns panic into peace of mind.

10 / WATER: STORE, FILTER, PURIFY

You can survive three weeks without food, but only **three days without water.** That's why, in any collapse scenario, water is your number one priority. Food shortages make life hard, but water shortages make life impossible.

When the dollar fails, supply chains fail with it. That means bottled water disappears from shelves overnight, utilities cut corners, and municipal water systems become unreliable. To keep your family safe, you need both **storage** and **purification** systems in place before crisis strikes.

STEP 1: HOW MUCH WATER DO YOU REALLY NEED?

The standard rule: **1 gallon per person per day.**

- Half a gallon for drinking.
- Half a gallon for cooking and hygiene.

For a family of 4:

- 1 day = 4 gallons.
- 14 days = 56 gallons.

- 30 days = 120 gallons.

Pets need water too: add at least **0.5–1 gallon per pet per day**.

STEP 2: STORAGE OPTIONS

Short-Term (Up to 2 Weeks)

- Store bottled water cases in a cool, dark area.
- Rotate every 12 months (check expiration dates).

Mid-Term (1–6 Months)

- 5–7 gallon water jugs with handles (easy to move).
- Stackable containers labeled "food-grade."

Long-Term (6+ Months)

- 55-gallon water barrels (use food-safe plastic, BPA-free).
- Underground cisterns or rainwater collection systems (where legal).

Tip: Always store water away from chemicals, gasoline, or cleaning products.

STEP 3: PURIFICATION METHODS

Stored water is only as safe as the container. In crisis, even "clean" sources may be contaminated. That's why purification is essential.

1. Boiling

- Bring water to a **rolling boil for 1 minute** (3 minutes at high altitude).
- Kills bacteria, viruses, and parasites.

2. Bleach Treatment

- Use **unscented household bleach** (5–6% sodium hypochlorite).

- Add **8 drops per gallon** of clear water, stir, and wait 30 minutes.
- If water is cloudy, double the dose (16 drops per gallon).

3. Water Filters

- Portable filters (LifeStraw, Sawyer Mini, Berkey).
- Remove sediment, bacteria, and protozoa.
- Some models also reduce heavy metals.

4. UV Purifiers

- Battery or solar-powered UV devices.
- Destroy microbes if water is clear.

5. Rainwater Collection

- Use gutters and food-grade barrels.
- Always filter and disinfect before drinking.

STEP 4: BACKUP & REDUNDANCY

Never rely on just one method. A solid plan has:

- Stored water for at least 2 weeks.
- Filters for resupply.
- Bleach or tablets as last-resort backup.

STEP 5: QUICK ACTION PLAN

1 Calculate water needs for your household.

2 Start with bottled water for 2 weeks.

3 Add larger containers for 1–6 months.

4 Learn and practice at least **two purification methods.**

5 Review and rotate supplies every 6–12 months.

In a collapse, water is life. With a smart storage plan and multiple purification options, your family won't be among the millions left thirsty, desperate, and vulnerable.

Preparedness starts with water — everything else comes second.

11 / BACKUP POWER & HEAT

IF THE DOLLAR COLLAPSES, power companies won't be immune. Rising fuel costs, disrupted supply chains, and maintenance cuts can all lead to **rolling blackouts** or complete grid failures. We've seen it before — from California wildfires to Texas freezes — millions of families suddenly plunged into darkness.

When the grid goes down, your survival depends on how well you've prepared your **backup energy systems.** This doesn't mean you need to live off solar panels in the desert. It means having reliable tools to keep your essentials running when the power is gone.

STEP 1: KNOW YOUR PRIORITIES

You don't need to power your whole house. Focus on **mission-critical needs:**

- **Lighting** (flashlights, lanterns, headlamps).
- **Communication** (phones, radios).
- **Refrigeration** (medications, some food).
- **Heat or Cooling** (at least one safe backup method).

- **Basic cooking** (camp stove, propane burner).

Write a list of what your family truly can't live without for 72 hours, then expand to two weeks.

STEP 2: LEVELS OF BACKUP POWER

Level 1: Basic Emergency Power

- Flashlights, headlamps, and LED lanterns.
- Battery banks for phones.
- Rechargeable batteries with a small solar charger.

Level 2: Intermediate Backup

- Gas or propane generator (2,000–5,000 watts).
- Enough fuel for 3–7 days.
- Extension cords or transfer switch for appliances.

Level 3: Long-Term Resilience

- Solar panels with battery storage (small portable kits to large home systems).
- Inverter generators (quiet, fuel-efficient).
- Wood stove or rocket stove for heat and cooking.

STEP 3: FUEL STORAGE & SAFETY

- Store gasoline in **approved containers**, away from living spaces.
- Add fuel stabilizer for long-term storage.
- Rotate every 6–12 months.
- Propane tanks last indefinitely if stored properly.

Rule of Thumb: Always keep **at least 1 week of fuel** for your generator or stove.

STEP 4: NON-ELECTRIC BACKUPS

Some solutions don't require electricity at all:

- **Hand-crank radios** and flashlights.
- **Gravity-fed water filters** (like Berkey).
- **Manual tools** (can openers, grinders, saws).
- **Wood stoves** for heating and cooking.

These low-tech options ensure that even if batteries fail, you're still functional.

STEP 5: FAMILY BLACKOUT DRILL

A fun but powerful exercise:

1 Turn off your breaker for 24 hours.

2 Try living with only your backup systems.

3 Take notes: what worked, what failed, what was missing.

This test reveals gaps you'd never notice until it's too late.

STEP 6: QUICK START CHECKLIST

✓ Flashlights + batteries for each family member

✓ Power banks fully charged

✓ Generator + at least 1 week of fuel

✓ Backup cooking method (propane, wood, or solar)

✓ Battery or hand-crank radio

✓ Warm blankets and extra clothing

You don't need to live off-grid to survive a blackout. With layered backup systems — from flashlights to generators to solar panels — you can keep your family safe, comfortable, and confident even when the grid goes dark.

Preparedness is not about powering everything. It's about powering **what matters most.**

12 / HOME SECURITY IN UNSTABLE TIMES

WHEN MONEY LOSES VALUE, desperation rises. And with desperation comes crime. History proves it: during economic collapse, burglary, looting, and home invasions spike dramatically. Protecting your home base means more than food and water — it means securing what you've prepared against those who might try to take it.

The goal is not to turn your house into a fortress, but to make it a **hard target**. Criminals usually look for the easiest opportunity. With a few smart upgrades, you can make your home the one they skip.

STEP 1: THE THREATS YOU FACE

In unstable times, the most common dangers are:

- **Burglary:** Opportunistic thieves looking for food, cash, or valuables.

- **Looting:** Mobs targeting stores or neighborhoods during unrest.

- **Home Invasion:** Desperate people breaking in when they believe supplies are inside.

- **Theft of Supplies:** Opportunistic stealing of food, fuel, or tools from your yard or garage.

STEP 2: COMMON WEAK POINTS IN HOMES

Here are the areas criminals target most — and how to fix them:

1. Doors

- Weak locks or hollow-core doors are easy to kick in.
- **Fix:** Install solid-core or steel exterior doors. Add deadbolts, reinforced strike plates, and door jammers.

2. Windows

- Easy entry point, especially in basements or ground floors.
- **Fix:** Add window locks, shatter-resistant film, security bars (discreet designs available).

3. Garages

- Often overlooked, yet a major weak point.
- **Fix:** Use reinforced locks, disable electronic openers if power fails, secure tools/fuel inside.

4. Fences & Yards

- Low fences or poorly lit yards invite intruders.
- **Fix:** Motion sensor lights, thorny bushes under windows, and "defensive landscaping."

5. Visibility

- Supplies visible through windows or in plain sight.
- **Fix:** Keep blinds closed, blackout curtains for nighttime, store supplies discreetly.

STEP 3: LAYERS OF SECURITY

The best defense is a **layered system:**

1 Deterrence (Make Them Think Twice):

○ Motion lights, cameras (real or dummy), alarm signs.

2 Delay (Make Entry Difficult):

○ Strong locks, reinforced doors, window bars.

3 Defense (Protect Your Family):

○ Dogs, non-lethal deterrents, or firearms (if trained and legal in your state).

4 Plan (What If They Get In?):

○ Safe room or rally point for your family.

○ Communication plan (call police, contact neighbors).

STEP 4: COMMUNITY & AWARENESS

Security is not just hardware — it's relationships.

- **Know your neighbors.** A trusted community watches out for each other.

- **Neighborhood watch** or informal patrols can deter looters.

- **Situational awareness:** Train yourself and your family to notice unusual activity.

STEP 5: QUICK ACTION CHECKLIST

✓ Reinforce exterior doors with deadbolts and strike plates

✓ Install motion-sensor lights at entry points

✓ Apply shatter-resistant film to ground-level windows

- ✓ Secure garage doors and windows
- ✓ Store supplies out of sight (garage, basement, opaque bins)
- ✓ Create a safe room with a secondary exit if possible
- ✓ Build a communication plan with family and neighbors

Your home doesn't need to look like a fortress — but it does need to act like one. By addressing weak points and adding layers of security, you can turn your home into a place where your family feels safe, even as instability rises outside.

Preparedness isn't just about food and water. It's about defending the people and supplies that give you the strength to survive.

13 / MEDICAL & HYGIENE READINESS

IN A COLLAPSE, the medical system is often one of the first to fail. Hospitals overflow, pharmacies close, and even small injuries can turn deadly if untreated. A simple cut can become an infection, a fever can spiral, and poor hygiene can spread disease quickly.

Preparedness is not only about food and water — it's about keeping your family healthy when doctors and medicine are out of reach. That means building **medical kits, hygiene systems, and basic skills** to manage health at home.

STEP 1: THE ROLE OF MEDICAL PREPAREDNESS

- **Prevention first:** Hygiene and sanitation prevent most illnesses.

- **Immediate care:** Having supplies on hand to stop bleeding, disinfect wounds, and manage pain can save lives.

- **Chronic conditions:** If you or family members rely on medication, advance planning is non-negotiable.

STEP 2: THE MINI MEDICAL KIT (GO-BAG ESSENTIALS)

This is your **72-hour medical survival kit**, light enough to carry in a backpack:

- Adhesive bandages (various sizes)
- Sterile gauze pads & medical tape
- Antiseptic wipes & antibiotic ointment
- Elastic bandage (ACE wrap)
- Tweezers & small scissors
- Pain relievers (ibuprofen, acetaminophen)
- Allergy tablets (antihistamines)
- Rehydration salts or electrolyte packets
- Personal prescriptions (3-day supply minimum)
- Disposable gloves & CPR mask
- Hand sanitizer & travel soap
- Emergency blanket

Purpose: Treat small cuts, burns, fevers, allergic reactions, and dehydration until advanced care is available.

STEP 3: THE HOME MEDICAL KIT (ADVANCED SUPPLIES)

For long-term survival at home, expand to a more complete kit:

- Everything in the mini-kit, plus:
- Large trauma dressings & tourniquet
- Suture kit or butterfly bandages (if trained)
- Thermometer (digital + backup manual)

- Cold packs & heat packs
- Blood pressure monitor
- Antifungal cream & anti-diarrheal meds
- Cough syrup & decongestants
- Spare eyeglasses / contact supplies
- Dental kit (temporary fillings, clove oil)
- Antibiotics (if legally obtained through a doctor)
- Extra 30–90 days of personal medications
- Reference guide (First Aid Manual, printed)

Purpose: Handle more serious wounds, stabilize emergencies, and manage ongoing illnesses when hospitals are not an option.

STEP 4: HYGIENE & SANITATION

Illness spreads fast when sanitation fails. Keep these essentials:

- Soap, hand sanitizer, wet wipes.
- Toothbrushes, toothpaste, floss.
- Feminine hygiene products.
- Diapers and baby wipes (if needed).
- Trash bags, heavy-duty gloves, bleach for disinfection.
- Bucket + heavy bags (makeshift toilet if plumbing fails).

Golden Rule: *Stay clean, stay healthy.*

STEP 5: SKILLS MATTER MORE THAN STUFF

Even the best kit is useless without knowledge. Invest time in:

- A basic first aid/CPR course (Red Cross, local fire department).

- Online or book-based learning for wound care and infection control.

- Practicing drills: bandaging, splinting, using your own supplies.

STEP 6: QUICK ACTION CHECKLIST

✔ Mini-kit in every go-bag

✔ Advanced home kit in a secure location

✔ At least 30 days of prescriptions on hand

✔ Hygiene supplies stocked for 1–3 months

✔ First aid and CPR training completed

A medical emergency in a collapse is not the time to start learning. By building both a **portable mini-kit** and a **comprehensive home kit**, plus maintaining hygiene supplies and basic training, you give your family the tools to survive not just shortages — but sickness.

In survival, health is strength. Protect it, and your family stands a far better chance.

14 / KEEPING MORALE & MENTAL STRENGTH

When people think of survival, they picture stockpiled food, water filters, and backup power. But one of the most powerful tools for survival isn't stored in your basement — it's in your mind.

History shows that in every crisis, from wars to natural disasters, those who survived weren't always the strongest or the most prepared with gear. They were the ones who could **stay calm, adapt, and keep moving forward** even when fear, stress, and exhaustion tried to take over.

In a dollar collapse, uncertainty will be constant. News will be confusing, neighbors may panic, and daily routines will break down. That's when **mental resilience and morale** become your most valuable resources.

STEP 1: WHY MENTAL STRENGTH MATTERS

- **Fear spreads faster than fire.** If you panic, your family panics.

- **Decisions under stress** determine whether you waste resources or use them wisely.

- **Morale is contagious.** A calm leader gives confidence to everyone else.

Survival isn't just about calories and gallons. It's about keeping your spirit steady when everything around you shakes.

STEP 2: PRACTICAL STRESS-MANAGEMENT TOOLS

These are simple, low-tech strategies that anyone can practice daily:

- **Breathing Technique (Box Breathing):** Inhale for 4 counts, hold for 4, exhale for 4, hold for 4. Repeat for 2–3 minutes. Calms the nervous system.

- **Grounding Technique (5-4-3-2-1):** Notice 5 things you see, 4 things you feel, 3 things you hear, 2 you smell, 1 you taste. Brings the mind back to the present.

- **Routine Reset:** Even in chaos, keep regular times for meals, rest, and family check-ins. Structure reduces stress.

- **Movement & Exercise:** Push-ups, squats, stretches, walking. Physical activity reduces tension and keeps you strong.

- **Journaling:** Writing worries and plans clears the mind and prevents negative spirals.

STEP 3: FAMILY MORALE BOOSTERS

Survival is not just an individual game — it's a family mission. To keep spirits up:

- **Family Meetings:** Daily 5–10 minutes to update plans, share news, and reassure.

- **Simple Games:** Deck of cards, board games, or word games. Keeps children calm.

- **Music & Stories:** Singing, telling family stories, or reading aloud keeps hope alive.

- **Small Comforts:** Chocolate, tea, or favorite snacks boost morale beyond calories.

STEP 4: THE LEADERSHIP FACTOR

In every family or group, someone becomes the anchor. That doesn't mean barking orders — it means:

- Staying calm when others panic.

- Listening and reassuring.

- Making clear, confident decisions.

- Keeping focus on solutions, not just problems.

Your calmness is the shield your family needs.

STEP 5: QUICK ACTION CHECKLIST

✓ Practice at least one stress-reduction exercise daily

✓ Keep a routine (meals, rest, communication) even in chaos

✓ Include games, books, or small comforts in your supplies

✓ Hold daily family check-ins to build unity

✓ Lead with calmness, not fear

Supplies keep your body alive. **Morale keeps your spirit alive.** In a collapse, fear and despair can be deadlier than hunger. By practicing mental strength techniques, maintaining routines, and boosting family morale, you ensure that your household not only survives — but endures with dignity and hope.

PART IV — MOBILITY & COMMUNICATION

Preparedness doesn't end at your front door. In a collapse, there may come a moment when you must leave home — whether to reach safer ground, retrieve supplies, or meet with family. At the same time, when phone networks are down and the internet is unreliable, **staying in touch becomes as critical as food or water.**

Mobility and communication are about **freedom and connection.** If you can move safely, you're not trapped. If you can communicate, you're not isolated. Together, these skills ensure you're never powerless, even in unstable times.

In this section, you'll learn how to:

• Build a **bug-out bag** for fast evacuation.

• Plan escape routes and alternative travel methods when roads are blocked or fuel is scarce.

• Use maps, compasses, and navigation basics without relying on GPS.

• Stay connected with family and allies through radios, codes, and backup communication systems.

- Create a family mobility and communication plan so no one is left behind.

Your home is your fortress, but your **mobility is your lifeline.** And communication — whether it's a two-way radio, a written message, or a simple meeting point — is what keeps your family united when the world feels like it's falling apart.

By the end of this part, you'll know how to move, where to go, and how to stay connected no matter what happens.

15 / WHEN PHONES GO DEAD

IN EVERY MAJOR DISASTER, one of the first systems to fail is communication.

Cell towers overload, internet cuts out, and suddenly the devices we rely on daily — our phones — become useless. Without communication, panic spreads faster, families get separated, and coordination breaks down.

The good news: **you don't need the cell network to stay connected.** There are simple, reliable tools that preppers, hikers, and even truck drivers have used for decades to talk when phones go dead.

STEP 1: NOAA WEATHER RADIOS — YOUR LIFELINE TO INFORMATION

The **NOAA Weather Radio** is more than a forecast tool. In a collapse, it becomes your direct line to government emergency alerts.

• **What it provides:** Severe weather warnings, disaster alerts, public safety updates.

• **How it works:** Broadcasts 24/7 on dedicated frequencies across the U.S.

- **Best choice:** Battery-powered or hand-crank models with solar backup.

 Tip: Buy a model with SAME (Specific Area Message Encoding), so you only receive alerts for your county instead of constant nationwide noise.

STEP 2: FRS & GMRS RADIOS — SHORT-RANGE COMMUNICATION

Family Radio Service (FRS) and **General Mobile Radio Service (GMRS)** are handheld walkie-talkie style radios perfect for local communication.

- **FRS:**

  o Free to use, no license required.

  o Range: 1–2 miles (more in open areas).

  o Ideal for families or small groups nearby.

- **GMRS:**

  o Requires a simple FCC license (covers your whole family).

  o Range: Up to 5–10 miles with handhelds; more with repeaters.

  o Better penetration through buildings and terrain.

 Use Case: Perfect for staying in touch during neighborhood patrols, bug-out convoys, or family members scattered within a town.

STEP 3: HAM RADIO BASICS — LONG-RANGE & SERIOUS PREPAREDNESS

If you want true resilience, **ham radio (amateur radio)** is the gold standard. With it, you can communicate across states — even across countries — when all else fails.

- **License Needed:** The FCC requires testing, but Technician Class licenses are relatively easy to earn.

- **Equipment:** Handheld "HT" radios (like Baofeng UV-5R) cost as little as $30. Base stations and antennas extend range.

- **Capabilities:**

  o Short-range (local nets).

  o Long-range (HF bands can bounce signals off the atmosphere).

  o Emergency networks (ARES, RACES) often mobilize during crises.

  Why it matters: In Venezuela's collapse, ham operators kept families connected when phones and internet went dark.

STEP 4: LAYERED COMMUNICATION STRATEGY

Just like food and energy, communication needs redundancy:

1 **NOAA Radio** → for incoming alerts.

2 **FRS/GMRS** → for local family/group coordination.

3 **Ham Radio** → for long-distance contact and serious networking.

This layered approach ensures you're never fully cut off.

STEP 5: QUICK ACTION CHECKLIST

✓ Buy a NOAA weather/emergency radio with SAME alerts

✓ Keep a set of FRS radios charged for family use

✓ Consider a GMRS license and radios for greater range

✓ Start learning ham basics (study guides, local clubs, practice nets)

✓ Store spare batteries, solar chargers, and hand-cranks

When phones go dead, the unprepared are silenced. But with radios — NOAA for alerts, FRS/GMRS for local chatter, and ham for long-distance resilience — your family stays informed, connected, and one step ahead of the chaos.

Communication is not a luxury in crisis. It's survival.

16 / NAVIGATION WITHOUT GPS

Today, most people rely entirely on GPS. But in a collapse, cell networks can go down, satellites can be disrupted, and your phone's battery may simply die. When that happens, the ability to navigate with **maps, compasses, and natural cues** becomes essential.

Without navigation skills, you risk wasting energy, missing safe routes, or walking into danger zones. With them, you gain freedom — the power to move safely, find resources, and reconnect with loved ones.

STEP 1: THE PAPER MAP ADVANTAGE

Digital maps are convenient, but **paper never runs out of batteries**.

Every household should own:

- **Road atlas** of your state and neighboring states.

- **Topographic maps** of your local area (showing terrain, rivers, trails).

- **Printed city maps** with street details, especially if you live in urban areas.

☞ Store them in a waterproof case or zip bag. Highlight evacuation routes, hospitals, and safe meeting points in advance.

STEP 2: COMPASS BASICS

A compass is one of the simplest and most reliable navigation tools.

- **Parts to Know:** Baseplate, direction-of-travel arrow, rotating bezel, magnetic needle.

- **How to Use:**

1 Hold it flat and steady.

2 Turn bezel so "N" aligns with the red needle.

3 Follow the direction-of-travel arrow.

☞ Practice in your neighborhood before you need it in crisis.

STEP 3: LANDMARKS & NATURAL NAVIGATION

If you're caught without tools, nature still points the way.

- **Sun & Shadows:** The sun rises in the east, sets in the west. A stick shadow test can give you rough directions.

- **Stars:** The North Star (Polaris) always marks true north in the Northern Hemisphere.

- **Terrain Features:** Rivers usually lead to settlements. Power lines often follow roads. Hills and valleys can orient you on a map.

STEP 4: BUILDING A ROUTE PLAN

Never just "head out." Create a **route plan** before leaving:

- **Primary Route:** Fastest way to your destination.

- **Secondary Route:** Backup if the first is blocked.

- **Tertiary Route:** Off-road or footpath option.

Mark safe zones (friends' houses, safe gas stations, hospitals) along the way.

STEP 5: PRACTICE NOW, NOT LATER

Navigation is a perishable skill. To build confidence:

- Take short hikes using only a paper map and compass.
- Practice plotting routes on a topographic map.
- Teach children basic "point to north" skills.
- Run a "no-GPS day" where you navigate only with maps.

STEP 6: QUICK ACTION CHECKLIST

✓ Buy a reliable compass and learn to use it

✓ Stock road atlas + topo maps in waterproof bag

✓ Pre-mark evacuation routes and meeting points

✓ Learn basic sun, shadow, and star navigation

✓ Practice with family in safe settings

GPS is a convenience. Maps and compasses are freedom. In a collapse, those who can navigate will find safety, resources, and opportunities — while those who can't may end up lost, stranded, or worse.

By mastering old-school navigation, you ensure that **no blackout, no dead battery, and no system failure can trap you.**

17 / BUG-OUT VEHICLES & FUEL PLANNING

IN AN ECONOMIC COLLAPSE, there may come a time when staying put is no longer safe. Looting spreads, neighborhoods destabilize, or resources run out. That's when your **bug-out vehicle (BOV)** becomes your lifeline — the machine that can carry your family, supplies, and hope to safer ground.

But here's the catch: in crisis, roads clog, fuel disappears, and unprepared vehicles break down. That's why planning your transportation now is just as important as storing food and water.

STEP 1: WHAT MAKES A GOOD BUG-OUT VEHICLE?

The perfect BOV doesn't need to be a military truck or an armored SUV. It needs to be:

- **Reliable:** Regularly maintained, with a strong service history.

- **Fuel-Efficient:** Every gallon will matter in a crisis.

- **Capable:** Handles rough terrain or detours if main roads are blocked.

- **Spacious:** Enough room for your family and at least 72 hours of supplies.

- **Low-Profile:** Doesn't scream "prepper" or attract attention.

☞ Common choices:

- Pickup trucks (durable, cargo space).

- SUVs (capacity, off-road ability).

- Minivans (less glamorous, but huge storage).

- Motorcycles/bikes (great backup for weaving through traffic).

STEP 2: FUEL STORAGE & ROTATION

When the dollar collapses, gas stations may close or only accept cash. Fuel becomes currency.

- **Gasoline Storage:** Use approved fuel cans, add stabilizer, and rotate every 6–12 months.

- **Diesel Advantage:** Lasts longer in storage and often more available during shortages.

- **Propane:** Excellent for cooking and some generators, stores indefinitely.

Rule of Thumb: Always keep at least **one full tank + 20 extra gallons** in storage at home.

STEP 3: ESSENTIAL VEHICLE GEAR

Every bug-out vehicle should carry:

- Full spare tire, jack, and repair kit

- Jumper cables or jump starter pack

- Extra motor oil and coolant

- Tow straps and shovel
- Portable air compressor
- Maps (in glovebox)
- Fire extinguisher
- Emergency supplies: water, food bars, blankets, first aid kit

STEP 4: ROUTE & FUEL PLANNING

Don't just load up and drive. Think strategically:

- **Primary Route:** Fastest way out of your area.
- **Secondary Route:** Backroads, avoiding highways.
- **Tertiary Route:** Off-road or walking fallback.
- **Fuel Caches:** If possible, pre-position fuel along your bug-out route (trusted friend's property, hidden storage).

☞ Pro Tip: Calculate your vehicle's range (miles per gallon × tank size). Then plan your bug-out route within 75% of that distance to allow margin.

STEP 5: FAMILY MOBILITY DRILLS

A vehicle is only useful if your family knows how to use it in crisis. Practice:

- Packing your vehicle quickly (time yourself).
- Driving your primary and secondary routes.
- Switching drivers if the main driver is incapacitated.

STEP 6: QUICK ACTION CHECKLIST

- ✔ Choose and maintain a reliable, fuel-efficient vehicle
- ✔ Keep at least 1 full tank + 20 gallons stored at home
- ✔ Add fuel stabilizer and rotate supplies annually
- ✔ Equip vehicle with essential repair & survival gear
- ✔ Pre-plan multiple escape routes and practice them
- ✔ Run family bug-out drills twice a year

Your bug-out vehicle is not just transportation — it's survival on wheels. With the right planning, fuel reserves, and practice, you'll never be trapped by empty gas stations, gridlock, or breakdowns.

In crisis, mobility is freedom. And a ready vehicle means you hold the keys to escape when others are stuck.

18 / GRAB-AND-GO READINESS

IN A CRISIS, speed saves lives. Fires spread, unrest grows, floods rise, and sometimes you can't stay home no matter how well-stocked your pantry is. That's when **grab-and-go readiness** makes the difference between a smooth evacuation and a chaotic scramble.

Prepared families don't waste time searching for shoes, passports, or flashlights. They already have their gear packed, their vehicles stocked, and their evacuation drills practiced. When danger hits, they just grab their bags — and go.

STEP 1: THE GO-BAG (PERSONAL BUG-OUT BAG)

Every family member should have a backpack ready to cover **72 hours of survival**.

Essentials:

- Water (bottles or pouches, plus filter or LifeStraw)
- 3 days of non-perishable food (bars, trail mix, jerky)
- First aid kit + personal meds
- Flashlight + spare batteries

- Multi-tool or knife
- Fire starter (matches, lighter, ferro rod)
- Clothing layers + poncho
- Blanket or bivvy sack
- Hygiene items (toothbrush, wipes, sanitizer)
- Copies of IDs + small cash stash
- Phone charger + power bank
- Whistle, duct tape, paracord

Tip: Personalize each bag for children (comfort items, snacks) and pets (food, leash, vaccination records).

STEP 2: THE CAR KIT

If you evacuate by vehicle, your car is your rolling survival pod. Always keep a **basic car kit** in the trunk.

Essentials:

- Extra water and food bars
- Jumper cables and tire repair kit
- Blankets and spare clothing
- Flashlight and road flares
- Map + compass
- First aid kit
- Fuel canister (empty, ready to refill)
- Cash in small bills
- Portable stove or cooking kit (optional)

☞ Keep your gas tank at least **half full at all times.** In crisis, gas stations may shut down or have mile-long lines.

STEP 3: THE FAMILY EVACUATION BINDER

Beyond gear, you need your **critical documents in one place:**

- Birth certificates, IDs, passports
- Insurance policies
- Home deeds, vehicle titles
- Medical records & prescriptions
- Emergency contacts list
- Family photos (for identification)

☞ Store this in a waterproof pouch inside one of the go-bags.

STEP 4: EVACUATION DRILLS

Gear is useless without practice. Once your bags and car kits are ready, train like you mean it.

- **Drill 1: Grab-and-Go Speed Test**
  - Start timer. Family has 5 minutes to grab bags and load vehicle.
  - Goal: Out of driveway in under 10 minutes.
- **Drill 2: Route Familiarization**
  - Drive both primary and secondary evacuation routes.
  - Note choke points, fuel stops, and safe zones.
- **Drill 3: Night or Low-Visibility Scenario**
  - Practice grabbing bags and moving in darkness with flashlights.
  - Builds confidence for real emergencies.

STEP 5: QUICK ACTION CHECKLIST

✓ Go-bag for every family member (72-hour supply)

✓ Car kit with fuel, water, tools, and blankets

✓ Evacuation binder with critical documents

✓ Gas tank always kept half full or more

✓ Practice drills at least twice a year

When danger forces you to leave, hesitation can cost you everything. By preparing **go-bags, car kits, and evacuation drills** in advance, you turn panic into a plan.

Your home is your fortress — but your grab-and-go readiness is your parachute. When it's time to move, you'll move fast, confident, and together.

PART V — COMMUNITY & BARTER NETWORKS

No one survives collapse alone. Even the most well-stocked prepper eventually runs into limits: food runs low, skills fall short, or unexpected needs arise. History shows that in every crisis — from the Great Depression to Venezuela's currency crash — those who **thrived** weren't the isolated individuals, but the people who built strong communities and knew how to trade.

In a dollar collapse, cash may lose its power, but **trust and trade never will**.

Barter networks, skill-sharing, and community defense groups will become the new economy. The neighbor who knows how to fix engines, the family with extra chickens, or the person with medical training will all be more valuable than a pocket full of paper dollars.

This section will show you how to:

• Identify the allies you can trust — and avoid the ones you can't.

• Build small networks of mutual support (food, security, information).

• Develop **barter skills** and recognize which items will hold the most value when money fails.

- Protect yourself against exploitation or unfair trades.

- Strengthen your family's position by becoming a **provider, not just a consumer.**

Survival begins with self-reliance, but long-term survival depends on **community resilience.** By the end of this part, you'll know how to plug into local networks, trade wisely, and create alliances that protect and sustain your family in the hardest times.

19 / BUILDING TRUST IN CRISIS

In stable times, trust is easy. Banks hold your money, stores stock your food, police protect your neighborhood. But when those systems collapse, you're left to rely on **people — and your ability to judge who you can trust.**

During a dollar collapse, desperation will drive some to theft, fraud, or worse. But it will also bring out cooperation, generosity, and strength in others. The key to survival is learning how to **identify true allies** and avoid dangerous connections.

STEP 1: WHY TRUST IS SURVIVAL

- **No one has every skill.** You may have food, but someone else has medical knowledge.

- **Isolation is dangerous.** Lone households become easy targets.

- **Networks multiply strength.** Two families working together can watch, trade, and defend far more effectively.

Trust is the glue that makes survival possible.

STEP 2: SIGNS OF A RELIABLE ALLY

Not everyone is safe to bring into your circle. Look for people who show:

- **Consistency:** They do what they say, even in small matters.

- **Preparedness Mindset:** They already value planning and responsibility.

- **Reciprocity:** Willing to give as well as take.

- **Discretion:** They don't brag about your supplies or plans to outsiders.

- **Skills or Assets:** Medical, mechanical, gardening, security, or reliable resources.

Trust is built over time, but in crisis you'll need to read people quickly.

STEP 3: RED FLAGS OF A RISKY CONTACT

Avoid alliances with those who show:

- **Desperation:** They're constantly in need, never bringing value.

- **Dishonesty:** Even small lies are a warning sign.

- **Aggression:** Quick to anger, controlling, or manipulative.

- **Loose Lips:** If they gossip about others, they'll gossip about you.

One weak or reckless person can compromise your entire family's safety.

STEP 4: LAYERS OF TRUST

Trust isn't "all or nothing." Use layers:

1 **Outer Circle:** Acquaintances, neighbors, casual allies. Share only general info.

2 **Middle Circle:** Trusted partners for barter, security, or skill exchange. Share selective info.

3 **Inner Circle:** Family or bonded allies who know your plans and resources. Share deeply only here.

This layered approach prevents betrayal while still letting you cooperate.

STEP 5: BUILDING TRUST IN PRACTICE

• **Start Small:** Trade minor items or share small favors before larger commitments.

• **Prove Yourself:** Be reliable and consistent in return.

• **Set Boundaries:** Make clear what you will and won't share.

• **Use "Test Scenarios":** See how someone reacts under small pressure before relying on them in big ones.

STEP 6: QUICK ACTION CHECKLIST

✓ Identify potential allies in your neighborhood now

✓ Build trust gradually with small exchanges

✓ Watch for red flags (dishonesty, desperation, gossip)

✓ Keep inner-circle knowledge limited to those who've earned it

✓ Practice reciprocity — give and receive fairly

In a collapse, trust is your most valuable currency. With the right people, you gain strength, skills, and security far beyond what you can achieve alone. With the wrong people, you risk everything you've worked to build.

Learn to judge wisely, act carefully, and cultivate trust that can withstand the storm.

20 / BARTER BASICS — WHAT HOLDS VALUE WHEN MONEY DOESN'T

When the dollar loses its power, people won't stop needing food, medicine, or tools. The economy won't disappear — it will simply **shift** from paper currency to **barter and trade**. In every historical collapse — from Weimar Germany to Argentina — people found ways to exchange goods and skills directly, bypassing worthless money.

Understanding what holds value when cash fails is critical. Trade wisely, and you'll protect your family while strengthening your network. Trade poorly, and you risk losing what matters most.

STEP 1: THE NEW RULES OF VALUE

In crisis, value is measured not by price tags, but by **usefulness and scarcity**.

Ask:

- Does it meet a survival need (food, water, shelter, health, safety)?
- Is it difficult to find or replace?
- Can it be divided into smaller trades?

STEP 2: HIGH-VALUE BARTER ITEMS

These are the goods that consistently hold value when economies collapse:

- **Food Staples:** Rice, beans, pasta, flour, sugar, salt.

- **Water & Purification:** Bottled water, filters, purification tablets.

- **Fuel & Energy:** Propane canisters, firewood, batteries, candles, lighters.

- **Medicine & Hygiene:** Painkillers, antibiotics (if legal), soap, feminine products, diapers.

- **Tools & Gear:** Knives, flashlights, duct tape, multi-tools, paracord.

- **Comfort Items:** Coffee, tea, chocolate, tobacco, alcohol.

- **Defense:** Ammunition (where legal), pepper spray, whistles, sturdy locks.

☞ Even small luxuries like chocolate or cigarettes can have outsized value — because they provide comfort in dark times.

STEP 3: HIGH-VALUE SKILLS

Physical goods aren't the only tradable currency. Skills become priceless when systems collapse:

- **Medical Care:** First aid, dentistry, wound treatment.

- **Food Production:** Gardening, livestock care, food preservation.

- **Repair:** Mechanics, carpentry, sewing, electrical.

- **Protection:** Security, firearms training, patrol organization.

- **Teaching:** Literacy, tutoring, or skill training for children.

☞ A skill never runs out, never expires, and can be traded again and again.

STEP 4: HOW TO BARTER SAFELY

- **Start Small:** Test with minor trades before bigger exchanges.

- **Neutral Ground:** Meet in safe, public, or trusted areas.

- **Fair Exchange:** Always trade in items of real use, not just "luxury hype."

- **Diversify Stock:** Don't rely on one trade item — spread your resources.

- **Keep Quiet:** Don't advertise your full inventory.

STEP 5: AVOIDING PITFALLS

- **Don't Trade Away Essentials:** Never barter your last water, last medicine, or only defense tool.

- **Beware Counterfeits:** Fake meds, watered-down fuel, or broken tools.

- **Control Visibility:** If people know you have abundance, you may become a target.

STEP 6: QUICK ACTION CHECKLIST

✓ Start stocking small, tradable essentials (coffee, soap, lighters, meds)

✓ Develop at least one skill you can trade in crisis

✓ Practice small barters with friends or local farmers' markets

✓ Never trade away core survival items

✓ Keep discretion — your inventory is your security

. . .

When money dies, trade lives on. Goods and skills will form the backbone of a new economy, where survival value outweighs dollar value. By preparing barter items now — and sharpening skills that never expire — you'll be positioned not just to survive, but to thrive in the marketplace of crisis.

21 / SETTING UP A LOCAL EXCHANGE NETWORK

BARTER WORKS ONE-ON-ONE, but when communities organize, it becomes a **local economy**. In past collapses — from Argentina's 2001 crisis to small-town America during the Great Depression — people created **exchange networks** where neighbors could trade goods, skills, and services safely and fairly.

Setting up a local exchange network doesn't require a big organization or fancy systems. It starts small — with trust, structure, and a clear set of rules.

STEP 1: WHY NETWORKS WORK BETTER THAN LONE TRADES

- **Safety:** Trading in groups reduces the risk of scams or theft.

- **Efficiency:** More people means more variety of goods and skills.

- **Resilience:** Networks can continue even if individuals run out of items.

- **Community Strength:** Builds unity and mutual aid during hardship.

STEP 2: STARTING SMALL

Begin with your **trusted circle:** family, close friends, and reliable neighbors. Agree on a simple system:

- Meet weekly or bi-weekly.

- Bring items or skills available for trade.

- Keep trades fair and practical.

Think of it as a "survival farmer's market" where everyone contributes something.

STEP 3: CHOOSING A MEDIUM OF EXCHANGE

Barter doesn't always mean straight swaps. To keep things smoother, you can use:

- **Credit Ledger:** Track who owes what in a simple notebook.

- **Tokens/Chits:** Poker chips, printed notes, or marked coins representing value.

- **Skill Hours:** Trade based on time (e.g., one hour of carpentry = one hour of childcare).

The goal isn't perfection — it's fairness and function.

STEP 4: RULES FOR SAFETY & TRUST

Every network needs basic rules:

- **Neutral Meeting Place:** Church hall, community center, or a trusted yard.

- **Code of Conduct:** No threats, no theft, no fraud.

- **Transparency:** Trades are witnessed by others, reducing risk of cheating.

- **Exclusion Policy:** Anyone who breaks trust is removed immediately.

STEP 5: SCALING UP

Once your network is working, you can:

- Expand to nearby neighborhoods.
- Specialize (e.g., one family provides eggs, another repairs tools).
- Organize patrols or community defense as part of the group.

In time, your network can evolve into a **mutual aid society**, offering not just trade, but security, shared labor, and resilience.

STEP 6: QUICK ACTION CHECKLIST

✔ Start with 3–5 trusted families or neighbors

✔ Agree on meeting times and rules

✔ Choose a simple exchange system (ledger, tokens, skill hours)

✔ Keep trades transparent and witnessed

✔ Grow slowly, adding only trusted members

✔ Remove anyone who endangers trust

Barter keeps you alive. A barter **network** helps you thrive. By building small, trusted circles of exchange, you create not just an economy — but a community that can withstand crisis together.

Preparedness starts alone, but survival is strongest in numbers.

PART VI — LONG-TERM RESILIENCE

The first days and weeks of a collapse are about survival — keeping food on the table, water in the jug, and your family safe through the storm. But what happens when the crisis doesn't end quickly? What if the dollar never regains its strength, supply chains stay broken, and the "emergency" becomes the new normal?

That's where **long-term resilience** comes in.

This stage of preparedness isn't just about making it through the next week. It's about building systems that keep working for months, years, and even generations.

In this section, you'll discover how to:

• Establish **sustainable food systems** with gardening, livestock, and preservation.

• Build **renewable energy solutions** like solar, wood, and alternative fuels.

• Strengthen your home into a **self-reliant hub**, not just a storage space.

- Maintain **physical health and fitness** without relying on gyms or modern medicine.

- Develop the mindset of adaptability — turning survival into stability, and eventually into a new way of thriving.

Preparedness begins with storage and supplies. True resilience begins when you can **produce, repair, and renew** what you need instead of depending on fragile outside systems.

By the end of this part, you'll no longer see yourself as just surviving the collapse — but as building a new foundation for a stronger, more independent life.

22 / GROWING FOOD WHEN STORES ARE EMPTY

IN A COLLAPSE, the shelves empty in days. Trucks stop rolling, farms can't ship produce, and supermarkets become battle zones. That's why long-term survival depends on your ability to **grow your own food**. Even a small garden can make the difference between hunger and security.

Growing food isn't just about calories. It's about **independence, health, and trade**. Seeds become wealth, fresh vegetables prevent disease, and surplus crops become powerful barter items.

STEP 1: START SIMPLE, GROW SMART

If you're new to gardening, don't try to grow everything at once. Focus on **easy, reliable, high-yield crops** first:

- **Potatoes:** Calorie-dense, easy to store.
- **Beans:** Protein-rich, grow on small trellises.
- **Tomatoes:** High yield, good for sauces and drying.
- **Zucchini & Squash:** Grow abundantly with little care.
- **Leafy Greens:** Fast-growing, continuous harvest.

- **Herbs (basil, oregano, mint):** Compact, flavorful, and barter-friendly.

☞ Even a small raised bed or a few containers on a balcony can provide meaningful food.

STEP 2: KNOW YOUR SPACE

- **Urban:** Container gardens, vertical growing, window boxes.
- **Suburban:** Raised beds, backyard plots, small fruit trees.
- **Rural:** Full gardens, orchards, livestock integration.

Adapt the garden to the space you have, not the space you wish you had.

STEP 3: SOIL, SEEDS, AND SUNLIGHT

- **Soil:** Healthy soil is the foundation. Compost kitchen scraps and yard waste.
- **Seeds:** Buy heirloom or open-pollinated varieties so you can save seeds year after year.
- **Sunlight:** Most crops need at least 6–8 hours of full sun daily.

☞ Pro Tip: Keep a **seed bank** — vacuum-sealed or jarred — as insurance for future planting seasons.

STEP 4: PRESERVATION & STORAGE

Fresh food spoils fast, but with preservation, you stretch harvests through the year:

- **Canning:** Vegetables, fruits, sauces.
- **Drying/Dehydrating:** Herbs, fruits, jerky.
- **Fermenting:** Sauerkraut, pickles, yogurt.

- **Root Cellaring:** Store potatoes, carrots, onions in cool, dark areas.

Preservation turns seasonal abundance into year-round resilience.

STEP 5: TRADING SEEDS & CROPS

Seeds and produce aren't just food — they're currency. In a collapsed economy:

- Seeds = wealth for future harvests.
- Fresh produce = barter leverage against packaged goods.
- Herbs & spices = high value for both nutrition and comfort.

Building a network of local gardeners strengthens both food security and community resilience.

STEP 6: QUICK ACTION CHECKLIST

✓ Start a small, easy garden with 3–5 reliable crops

✓ Learn composting basics to keep soil fertile

✓ Store heirloom seeds for future planting

✓ Learn at least one preservation method (canning, drying, fermenting)

✓ Trade surplus produce and seeds with neighbors or networks

Food storage carries you through weeks. Food production carries you through years. With a small garden, preserved harvests, and seed-saving skills, you become less dependent on failing systems — and more capable of feeding your family in any crisis.

The future belongs to those who can grow.

23 / RAISING SMALL LIVESTOCK FOR PROTEIN

VEGETABLE GARDENS KEEP you alive with calories, fiber, and vitamins. But long-term survival also requires **protein and fat** — the building blocks of strength, energy, and immune function. In a collapse, meat, eggs, and dairy become luxuries on supermarket shelves. That's why raising small livestock is one of the smartest ways to secure nutrition for your family.

You don't need a big farm. Even in suburban backyards or rural edge plots, small animals can provide steady, renewable protein with minimal investment.

STEP 1: WHY SMALL LIVESTOCK WORKS

- **Efficient:** Converts scraps and grass into protein-rich food.
- **Scalable:** Works on small lots, patios, or backyards.
- **Renewable:** Animals reproduce and multiply over time.
- **Barter Value:** Eggs, milk, and meat are always in demand.

STEP 2: TOP CHOICES FOR SURVIVAL LIVESTOCK

Chickens

- **Benefits:** Eggs almost daily, meat if needed.
- **Space Needs:** Small coop + outdoor run.
- **Feed:** Kitchen scraps, grains, forage.
- **Barter Value:** Eggs are among the most tradable survival foods.

Rabbits

- **Benefits:** High-protein meat, very quiet animals.
- **Space Needs:** Hutches or cages, even indoors in a shed/garage.
- **Feed:** Grass, hay, veggies.
- **Barter Value:** Reproduce quickly — excellent trade animals.

Goats

- **Benefits:** Milk (drink, cheese, yogurt) and meat.
- **Space Needs:** Fenced yard or pasture, shelter from rain.
- **Feed:** Grass, weeds, brush — very adaptable.
- **Barter Value:** Goat milk and cheese carry high trade demand.

Ducks (Optional)

- **Benefits:** Eggs, meat, pest control in gardens.
- **Space Needs:** Coop + access to small pond or tub of water.
- **Barter Value:** Eggs last longer than chicken eggs, very resilient animals.

STEP 3: SHELTER & CARE BASICS

- **Housing:** Dry, ventilated, predator-proof.
- **Water:** Fresh water daily (especially for ducks and goats).
- **Feed:** Balance of forage, scraps, and stored grains.
- **Health:** Learn simple checks (eyes clear, coats glossy, active behavior).

STEP 4: SUSTAINABLE PRACTICES

- **Breeding Stock:** Keep a few males for long-term reproduction.
- **Rotation:** Use droppings as fertilizer for your garden (compost first).
- **Integration:** Animals + garden = closed food loop.

STEP 5: PROTEIN PRESERVATION

Animal products spoil quickly, so plan preservation:

- **Eggs:** Coat with mineral oil for room-temp storage.
- **Meat:** Freeze (if power available), smoke, or pressure-can.
- **Milk:** Transform into cheese or yogurt for longer shelf life.

STEP 6: QUICK ACTION CHECKLIST

✓ Start with chickens or rabbits (easiest for beginners)

✓ Build simple, predator-proof housing

✓ Learn to compost animal manure for garden use

✓ Keep a mix of males and females for breeding sustainability

✓ Master one preservation method for meat, milk, or eggs

・ ・ ・

Small livestock is a **renewable food source** that turns scraps and weeds into vital protein. Chickens, rabbits, and goats aren't just animals — they're resilience on legs. With them, your family gains independence from fragile supply chains and steady nutrition in times when others go hungry.

24 / RENEWABLE ENERGY SOLUTIONS

When the grid flickers, you can survive with candles, flashlights, and a generator for a few days. But if the collapse drags on for months or years, stored fuel will eventually run out. That's when renewable energy solutions become the backbone of long-term survival.

Renewables are not about "green politics" — they're about **freedom from dependency.** A family that can generate its own electricity, heat its own shelter, and cook without relying on outside supply is a family that can endure any crisis.

STEP 1: SOLAR POWER

• **Portable Solar Kits:** Small panels with battery packs to keep phones, radios, and lights running.

• **Home Solar Systems:** Roof or ground-mounted panels feeding into a battery bank (lithium or lead-acid).

• **DIY Solar Lighting:** Garden solar lights can be brought inside at night.

☞ Even a modest 200–400W solar system can power essential lights, radios, and a small freezer.

STEP 2: WOOD & BIOMASS

- **Wood Stoves:** Provide both heat and cooking power. Essential in colder climates.

- **Rocket Stoves:** Small, efficient stoves that use twigs and branches.

- **Pellet Stoves:** More efficient, but require stored pellets.

☞ Collecting wood also requires sustainable rotation to avoid stripping your land.

STEP 3: BIOGAS & ALTERNATIVE FUELS

- **Biogas Digesters:** Convert food scraps, manure, and organic waste into methane gas for cooking.

- **Biodiesel:** If you have the know-how, waste vegetable oil can be converted to fuel.

- **Alcohol Stoves:** Simple stills can produce ethanol for small cooking stoves (where legal).

STEP 4: HUMAN & MECHANICAL POWER

When electricity fails, muscle power becomes valuable again.

- **Hand-Crank Devices:** Radios, flashlights, even blenders.

- **Bicycles:** Transport, power (bike generators), barter asset.

- **Manual Tools:** Hand saws, grain grinders, pumps.

☞ A return to hand tools ensures work continues even when fuel and batteries vanish.

STEP 5: ENERGY MANAGEMENT & CONSERVATION

Producing energy is only half the battle — conserving it is just as important.

- Switch to **LED lighting**.

- Insulate rooms to reduce heating needs.

- Cook with efficient stoves instead of open fires.

- Use "energy zones" in your home (central heated room instead of whole house).

STEP 6: QUICK ACTION CHECKLIST

✓ Add a small solar kit with panels + battery bank

✓ Invest in a wood stove or rocket stove for cooking/heat

✓ Stockpile firewood or pellets (rotate yearly)

✓ Explore simple biogas or fuel alternatives if possible

✓ Keep manual tools as backup for powered ones

✓ Train your family in energy conservation habits

Fuel runs out. The grid breaks down. But the sun shines, the wind blows, and wood grows every year. By integrating renewable energy solutions — even small ones — you reduce dependence on failing systems and build true resilience for the long haul.

Survival isn't just about enduring the dark. It's about keeping the lights on when everyone else is left behind.

25 / PHYSICAL HEALTH & FITNESS FOR SURVIVAL

IN TIMES OF COLLAPSE, hospitals may be inaccessible, gyms closed, and medicine scarce. Your **body becomes your most important tool.** No amount of supplies can replace the strength to carry water, the endurance to chop wood, or the resilience to recover from illness.

Survival fitness is not about bodybuilding. It's about being **strong enough, fast enough, and healthy enough** to handle the physical demands of crisis life.

STEP 1: THE SURVIVAL FITNESS MINDSET

Forget six-packs and mirror muscles. Focus on:

- **Strength:** Lifting, carrying, pulling.
- **Endurance:** Walking, hiking, working long hours.
- **Mobility:** Flexibility to avoid injury.
- **Resilience:** A body that heals fast and resists illness.

STEP 2: FUNCTIONAL SURVIVAL EXERCISES

No gym required — just body weight and simple tools.

• **Push-Ups & Pull-Ups:** Build upper body strength for lifting and climbing.

• **Squats & Lunges:** Leg power for carrying loads and long hikes.

• **Planks & Core Work:** Stability for balance and injury prevention.

• **Farmer's Carries:** Practice carrying buckets, jugs, or firewood.

• **Rucking:** Walking with a weighted backpack to simulate bug-out loads.

Train with **real objects** — water jugs, logs, backpacks — to mimic survival tasks.

STEP 3: ENDURANCE TRAINING

Collapse life means **walking more, driving less.** Build stamina now:

• Daily brisk walks (30–60 minutes).

• Hiking with elevation if possible.

• Interval training: mix bursts of speed with steady movement.

STEP 4: NUTRITION FOR RESILIENCE

In survival, nutrition fuels recovery. Focus on:

• **Balanced Diet:** Protein for muscle, carbs for energy, fats for endurance.

• **Hydration:** Water first, electrolytes as needed.

• **Micronutrients:** Vitamins from garden produce or supplements.

☞ Avoid relying only on stored processed foods — fresh greens and protein sources are vital.

STEP 5: PREVENTIVE HEALTH HABITS

A healthy body avoids collapse from small problems.

- Maintain **healthy weight** (excess fat slows mobility).

- Keep **teeth and gums healthy** — dental issues can become severe without dentists.

- Stretch daily to prevent stiffness and injury.

- Sleep 7–8 hours when possible — fatigue kills judgment.

STEP 6: FAMILY FITNESS & TRAINING

Preparedness is not just for adults. Kids and elderly family members need tailored activity:

- **Kids:** Make hikes and chores fun — they'll build resilience without realizing.

- **Elders:** Focus on balance, light strength, and endurance walks.

☞ The stronger your family as a unit, the less likely someone becomes a burden in crisis.

STEP 7: QUICK ACTION CHECKLIST

✓ Train bodyweight strength 3–4 times a week

✓ Walk or hike daily to build stamina

✓ Practice carrying water, firewood, or supplies

✓ Keep balanced nutrition and hydration

✓ Maintain dental, joint, and sleep health

✔ Include kids and elders in family fitness

Your body is the one tool you can't replace. A strong, mobile, resilient body turns survival from struggle into confidence. In a collapse, being fit means you can carry your child, haul your water, chop your wood, and defend your home.

Preparedness begins with gear — but it succeeds with **strength.**

26 / ADAPTING TO THE NEW NORMAL

At first, collapse feels like chaos. Empty shelves, silent phones, powerless nights. But as weeks turn into months, people stop asking *"When will things go back to normal?"* and start realizing: *"This is the new normal."*

Survival is no longer about rationing for a few days. It's about building a lifestyle that works in the new reality — a world where the dollar no longer guarantees stability, and resilience replaces convenience.

STEP 1: SHIFT YOUR MINDSET

- **From Short-Term to Long-Term:** Stop waiting for rescue. Plan as if systems won't return soon.

- **From Consumer to Producer:** Grow, repair, and create more than you consume.

- **From Isolation to Integration:** A lone household survives weeks. A community survives years.

STEP 2: DAILY RHYTHMS OF RESILIENCE

New stability comes from routines:

- Morning: Water collection, animal care, garden check.
- Midday: Cooking, repairs, training, trading.
- Evening: Security checks, family meeting, rest.

Routine reduces stress and makes collapse life predictable.

STEP 3: REDEFINING WEALTH

In the new economy, wealth isn't paper or numbers on a screen. It's:

- **Skills:** The ability to fix, heal, grow, or teach.
- **Health:** A strong body and sound mind.
- **Community:** Allies who trust you and support your family.
- **Supplies & Systems:** Food, water, tools, and renewables that keep running.

STEP 4: PASSING KNOWLEDGE FORWARD

Resilience becomes stronger when it's generational. Teach children:

- Gardening, cooking, and preservation.
- Navigation, tool use, and basic repair.
- Morale-building and storytelling (hope is survival too).

  Knowledge that lives in people can never be stolen.

STEP 5: SIGNS YOU'VE ADAPTED

- You're no longer anxious when shelves are empty.

- Your family's meals come mostly from your own systems.
- You trade skills and goods as part of a community economy.
- You feel **confidence, not panic**, when the lights go out.

This is the true marker of resilience — not just surviving crisis, but mastering it.

STEP 6: QUICK ACTION CHECKLIST

✓ Accept that the "old normal" may not return

✓ Build sustainable daily routines around food, water, and energy

✓ Redefine wealth as skills, health, and trust — not dollars

✓ Pass knowledge to the next generation

✓ Celebrate milestones of progress — not just survival

Collapse doesn't have to mean despair. It can mean transformation. By adapting your mindset, routines, and community ties, you don't just survive the fall of the old system — you build the foundation of a stronger, freer life.

Preparedness begins in fear, but it ends in **confidence**.

PART VII – SPIRITUAL & MENTAL PREPAREDNESS

When shelves are empty, when the lights go out, when neighbors panic and the world feels broken — one thing decides whether you keep going: **your inner strength**.

Food, water, and security keep your body alive. But it's your **mindset and spirit** that keep you moving forward when exhaustion and fear set in. History shows that in wars, famines, and collapses, those who survived weren't always the strongest or the most prepared. They were the ones who refused to give up — who found meaning, faith, or discipline in the darkest nights.

This final section is about preparing the part of survival that no checklist can cover:

• How to manage **stress, fear, and uncertainty** without breaking.

• How to build **hope and morale** inside your family when despair spreads outside.

• How to use **faith, values, or personal purpose** as anchors in chaos.

• How to cultivate the kind of mental toughness that sees opportunity instead of only loss.

Preparedness is not just a physical act. It is a spiritual journey and a mental discipline. By mastering both, you don't just prepare to survive collapse — you prepare to **emerge from it stronger, wiser, and more resilient than ever before.**

27 / THE SURVIVAL MINDSET

When disaster strikes, most people focus on gear — food, water, flashlights. But the truth is, your **greatest survival tool is your mind.**

A well-stocked pantry won't save you if panic makes you freeze. A strong body won't matter if despair convinces you to quit. In every crisis, from war zones to natural disasters, the difference between life and death often comes down to **mindset**.

STEP 1: THE CORE OF A SURVIVAL MINDSET

Survivors share a few common traits. They:

- **Stay Calm Under Pressure:** Fear is natural, but panic kills.
- **Adapt Quickly:** When Plan A fails, they move to Plan B.
- **Refuse to Quit:** They focus on solutions, not on despair.
- **Lead by Example:** Their confidence stabilizes others.

This mindset is not genetic. It's a skill you can build.

STEP 2: HOW TO BUILD EMOTIONAL RESILIENCE

• **Discipline in Routine:** Set daily tasks (water, food, security) even in chaos. Structure brings calm.

• **Control What You Can:** Focus on actions, not fears. You can't control the collapse — but you can control how you prepare.

• **Stress Reset:** Use breathing, stretching, or prayer to calm your body before making decisions.

• **Mental Rehearsal:** Visualize crises and your response. When it happens, you'll be less shocked.

STEP 3: AVOIDING THE PANIC SPIRAL

Panic spreads fast — in crowds, families, even neighborhoods. To avoid it:

• **Slow Down:** Take one deep breath before any major decision.

• **Limit Overload:** Don't drown in rumors or constant bad news.

• **Anchor in Purpose:** Remind yourself *why* you must endure — for family, faith, or future.

STEP 4: TRAINING YOUR MIND DAILY

Just like muscles, mental toughness grows with use:

• **Cold Exposure:** Showers or winter walks teach you to endure discomfort.

• **Fasting:** Occasional skipped meals prepare your body and mind for scarcity.

• **Challenge Days:** Practice living without power, phones, or comfort for 24 hours.

- **Journaling:** Writing down thoughts clarifies fears and strengthens resolve.

STEP 5: FAMILY & GROUP MORALE

A calm leader creates a calm family. Build group resilience by:

- Keeping regular family meetings.
- Sharing hope as well as challenges.
- Encouraging everyone, even children, to contribute to survival tasks.
- Celebrating small wins (a successful meal, repaired tool, secure night).

STEP 6: QUICK ACTION CHECKLIST

✓ Practice calming techniques (breathing, prayer, meditation)

✓ Build routines for stability in uncertain times

✓ Train mind and body with small stress challenges

✓ Avoid panic by focusing on purpose and control

✓ Lead with calm confidence to anchor your family

Survival begins in the mind. Panic wastes resources. Discipline preserves them. Fear isolates you. Purpose unites you. With a trained survival mindset, you turn collapse into challenge — and challenge into victory.

The strongest weapon you carry isn't in your go-bag or your toolbox. It's the determination inside you to never give up.

28 / FAITH, PURPOSE & INNER STRENGTH

IN EVERY COLLAPSE, some people give up while others rise. Supplies help, skills help, but what truly sustains survivors is something deeper: **faith, purpose, and inner strength.**

When food is scarce, when fear presses in, when exhaustion makes you want to quit — it's not the strength of your arms that keeps you moving, it's the strength of your spirit.

STEP 1: WHY FAITH MATTERS IN CRISIS

Faith doesn't have to mean religion (though it can). It's about having an **anchor beyond the chaos** — a belief or higher value that gives meaning when everything else feels unstable.

- For some, it's trust in God.

- For others, it's a mission to protect their children.

- For others still, it's loyalty to community or principle.

Faith transforms suffering into purpose. Without it, despair wins.

STEP 2: DEFINING YOUR PURPOSE

Ask yourself: *"What do I live for when things get hard?"*

- Family?
- Service to others?
- Building a better tomorrow?

Write it down. Share it with your family. Let it guide decisions when fear clouds judgment.

STEP 3: INNER STRENGTH PRACTICES

Inner strength isn't abstract — it's built through habits:

- **Prayer or Meditation:** Daily reflection restores calm.
- **Gratitude Practice:** List three blessings, even in hardship.
- **Affirmations:** Speak courage into existence ("We will endure. We are prepared.").
- **Silence & Stillness:** Take moments each day to breathe, think, and reset.

STEP 4: PASSING STRENGTH TO FAMILY

Your strength multiplies when you share it:

- **Encourage, don't discourage.** Replace "We can't" with "Here's what we can do."
- **Model calm.** Children and spouses mirror your tone.
- **Celebrate faith rituals.** Reading scripture, sharing blessings, or storytelling builds hope.

STEP 5: STORIES OF RESILIENCE

History shows how faith carried people through:

• Prisoners of war survived years in camps by holding onto inner belief.

• Families in famine endured by focusing on future generations.

• Communities in disasters found strength through prayer and solidarity.

Faith doesn't erase suffering, but it gives the power to endure it.

STEP 6: QUICK ACTION CHECKLIST

✓ Write down your personal "survival purpose"

✓ Practice daily reflection (prayer, meditation, journaling)

✓ Share gratitude or blessings as a family

✓ Use affirmations to strengthen morale

✓ Anchor decisions in faith and values, not just fear

Collapse will test your body, but it will test your spirit even more. Faith and purpose are the invisible fuel that carry you through when everything else runs dry. With inner strength, you transform fear into determination and hardship into meaning.

In survival, supplies keep you alive. Faith gives you a reason to keep living.

29 / TEACHING RESILIENCE TO THE NEXT GENERATION

THE TRUE TEST of survival isn't just keeping yourself alive — it's preparing your children to thrive in a changed world. In a collapse, kids don't just need food and shelter. They need **strength, skills, and hope** to face the future with courage.

If we fail to teach them resilience, we risk raising a generation that survives the storm physically but collapses mentally. If we succeed, we pass on the most powerful survival tool of all: **the will to endure.**

STEP 1: WHY CHILDREN NEED MORE THAN PROTECTION

It's natural to want to shield kids from hardship. But complete sheltering makes them unprepared when they must stand on their own. Children who are **included in survival routines** learn confidence and responsibility.

Resilient kids:

- Feel useful, not helpless.

- Understand sacrifice and teamwork.

- Grow stronger under stress instead of breaking.

STEP 2: AGE-APPROPRIATE SURVIVAL LESSONS

• **Young Children (4–7):** Simple chores (watering plants, gathering kindling). Games that teach awareness (spotting landmarks, practicing "what would you do if…").

• **Older Children (8–12):** Basic first aid, helping cook, learning to use maps, safe use of tools.

• **Teens (13+):** More responsibility — fire starting, animal care, patrol rotations, barter practice.

Tailor tasks to build pride without overwhelming them.

STEP 3: BUILDING MENTAL STRENGTH IN KIDS

• **Routine = Security:** Keep regular mealtimes, chores, and family check-ins.

• **Honesty with Hope:** Don't hide the truth, but frame it with confidence: *"Things are hard, but we are prepared."*

• **Resilience Through Play:** Games, storytelling, and small competitions keep morale high.

• **Encouragement Over Fear:** Teach through patience, not panic.

STEP 4: PASSING DOWN VALUES

Hardship is easier when rooted in meaning. Teach children:

• Gratitude (appreciating even small comforts).

• Faith or family traditions that provide strength.

• Service (helping siblings, neighbors, or animals).

• Pride in survival skills (gardening, fire-making, tool use).

STEP 5: LEGACY THROUGH KNOWLEDGE

Books can burn, supplies can be stolen — but knowledge carried in people endures.

- Teach kids how to grow food, filter water, and build shelter.
- Encourage them to ask questions and practice alongside you.
- Make survival skills part of family identity, not just emergency drills.

STEP 6: QUICK ACTION CHECKLIST

✓ Involve children in age-appropriate chores and survival tasks

✓ Keep routines steady to create security in chaos

✓ Teach honesty, framed with hope and confidence

✓ Share family values, stories, and faith practices

✓ Train kids in practical skills — water, food, tools, first aid

Children aren't just passengers in survival — they're the future drivers. By teaching them resilience, skills, and hope, you ensure your family's strength doesn't end with you.

In crisis, a resilient child isn't a burden — they're a force multiplier. The strongest legacy you can leave is not your supplies, but your children's ability to carry survival forward.

PART VIII— THE 30-DAY STEP-BY-STEP PLAN

Up to this point, you've learned the strategies, skills, and systems needed to survive a dollar collapse. But knowledge without action is just theory. That's why this final section transforms everything you've learned into a **30-day, step-by-step action plan** — a blueprint to move you from "thinking about preparedness" to **living preparedness.**

Over the next month, you'll be guided through daily tasks that build on each other, covering:

• **Financial Protection:** Setting up cash reserves, banking structures, and emergency funds.

• **Food & Water Security:** Stockpiling smartly, starting your pantry, and securing clean water sources.

• **Home Readiness:** Reinforcing security, building emergency kits, and preparing your family for crises.

• **Mobility & Communication:** Packing go-bags, preparing vehicles, and setting family evacuation plans.

• **Community & Barter:** Identifying allies, gathering barter items, and practicing small trades.

- **Mental & Spiritual Resilience:** Strengthening mindset, routines, and family morale.

Each day focuses on a **clear, achievable step** — from organizing your documents to practicing an evacuation drill. By the end of 30 days, you won't just know how to survive collapse. You'll have a **fully operational survival system** in place, ready to protect your family no matter what happens.

This plan isn't about fear. It's about action, confidence, and control. In just one month, you'll go from vulnerable to resilient — from hoping things won't get worse to **knowing you can handle whatever comes.**

30 / WEEK 1: SECURE YOUR FINANCES

THE COLLAPSE of a currency doesn't happen all at once. It starts with cracks in the system — rising prices, failing banks, restricted withdrawals. If you wait until the headlines scream "panic," it's too late. That's why the very first step of your 30-day plan is to **secure your finances.**

This week is about making sure your money works for you now, while preparing for the moment when dollars lose their power. By the end of these 7 days, you'll know exactly how much liquid cash you need, how to structure your bank accounts, and how to keep your family protected from sudden restrictions.

DAY 1: ASSESS YOUR FINANCIAL EXPOSURE

• Write down every bank account, credit card, loan, and investment you currently have.

• Identify **where your money is** and how quickly you can access it.

• Note which accounts are insured (FDIC coverage) and which are not.

Checklist:

✓ List all accounts & balances

✓ Mark insured vs. uninsured funds

✓ Identify risks (large savings in one bank, uninsured investments, etc.)

DAY 2: BUILD A CASH BUFFER

Banks can close overnight, and ATMs can run dry.

- Withdraw at least **one to two weeks of living expenses in cash.**
- Store it safely (fireproof safe, hidden compartment).
- Use small bills ($5s, $10s, $20s) — easier to trade than large ones.

☞ **Checklist:**

✓ Withdraw emergency cash

✓ Break into small denominations

✓ Securely store at home

DAY 3: DIVERSIFY BANK ACCOUNTS

Don't keep all your eggs in one basket.

- Open a second account in a different bank or credit union.
- Keep balances under **FDIC insurance limits ($250,000 per depositor, per bank).**
- Set up automatic transfers to spread funds safely.

☞ **Checklist:**

✓ Two or more separate banks

✓ Stay under FDIC limits

✓ Track account access and online logins

DAY 4: ELIMINATE WEAK DEBT

In a collapse, debt becomes a trap.

- Pay down high-interest credit cards first.
- Cancel unnecessary lines of credit.
- If possible, refinance into lower, fixed-rate terms.

☞ **Checklist:**

✓ List all debts

✓ Prioritize high-interest ones

✓ Develop payoff or freeze strategy

DAY 5: STOCK A HARD ASSET STARTER KIT

Cash may lose value fast. Begin moving into small, tangible assets:

- Silver coins or small gold pieces (easy to trade).
- Gift cards for gas, groceries, or essentials.
- Prepaid debit cards as backup.

☞ **Checklist:**

✓ Acquire small silver/gold denominations

✓ Store a few essential gift cards

✓ Keep assets secure but accessible

DAY 6: CREATE A FINANCIAL ESCAPE FOLDER

Put all financial documents in one place:

- Account numbers, passwords (written backup in a safe).
- Loan documents, deeds, insurance policies.

- Emergency contact list (bank reps, insurance agents).

☞ **Checklist:**

✓ Gather documents

✓ Store in fireproof folder

✓ Keep one digital copy on encrypted drive

DAY 7: PRACTICE A "BANK FREEZE DRILL"

Test your readiness:

- Imagine your bank accounts are frozen tomorrow.

- Could you buy food, pay bills, or cover gas with cash and reserves?

- Adjust your buffer until you could last **at least 14 days** without access to banks.

☞ **Checklist:**

✓ Run freeze simulation

✓ Identify weak points

✓ Adjust cash & assets

END OF WEEK 1: YOUR FINANCIAL FOUNDATION

By now, you should have:

- A clear map of your financial exposure.

- Cash safely stored at home.

- Multiple bank accounts under FDIC limits.

- A plan to kill high-interest debt.

- A starter kit of hard assets.

- An escape folder with critical documents.

- Confidence that if banks close tomorrow, you can still function.

This financial foundation is the **bedrock of collapse survival.** Without it, every other prep becomes shaky. With it, you move into Week 2 ready to tackle **food and water security** — the next pillars of survival.

31 / WEEK 2: BUILD FOOD & WATER RESERVES

MONEY WON'T FILL an empty stomach. When the dollar weakens and supply chains crack, food and water become the **real currency**. Grocery stores can be stripped bare in hours, and bottled water disappears even faster.

This week is about building a **practical, sustainable food and water stockpile** that will keep your family alive through panic runs and shortages. By the end of these 7 days, you'll have a pantry that could feed your family for at least 30 days — and the means to secure clean water no matter what happens to the tap.

DAY 8: TAKE INVENTORY OF CURRENT SUPPLIES

- Go through your pantry and note what you already have.

- Separate food into **perishables (fresh, freezer)** vs. **non-perishables (canned, dry goods)**.

- Calculate how many meals you could realistically cover.

- **Checklist:**

- ✓ Write down all pantry/freezer items
- ✓ Estimate meals per family member
- ✓ Identify gaps (protein, carbs, fats, vitamins)

DAY 9: BUILD A 30-DAY PANTRY PLAN

- Focus on calorie-dense, long-shelf-life staples:
  - Rice, beans, pasta, oats, flour, sugar, salt.
  - Canned meats (tuna, chicken, spam), canned vegetables & fruit.
  - Peanut butter, powdered milk, cooking oil.
- Create a **simple meal rotation** to avoid waste.
- **Checklist:**
- ✓ Buy or stock 30 days of staples
- ✓ Balance carbs, protein, fats
- ✓ Include comfort foods (coffee, chocolate, spices)

DAY 10: ADD READY-TO-EAT EMERGENCY FOODS

If power goes out, cooking may be impossible.

- Add items that require no cooking: granola bars, jerky, crackers, trail mix, MREs (Meals Ready-to-Eat).
- Store at least **3 days of "grab-and-go" food per person.**
- **Checklist:**
- ✓ Stock no-cook foods
- ✓ Include portable snacks for go-bags
- ✓ Label and rotate regularly

DAY 11: SECURE A WATER RESERVE

- Minimum: **1 gallon per person per day** for 14 days.
- Store in food-grade containers, bottled water, or large drums.
- Rotate every 6–12 months.

✒ **Checklist:**

✓ Store at least 14 gallons per family member

✓ Use clean, food-safe containers

✓ Keep water in a cool, dark space

DAY 12: WATER PURIFICATION BACKUP

Stored water runs out eventually. Plan for renewal.

- Portable filters (LifeStraw, Sawyer Mini).
- Water purification tablets or drops.
- Boiling setup (camp stove, fire, or rocket stove).

✒ **Checklist:**

✓ 2+ purification methods per household

✓ Train family members how to use them

✓ Store tablets/filters in go-bags too

DAY 13: ORGANIZE & ROTATE YOUR PANTRY

- Use the **FIFO method** (First In, First Out). Oldest food gets eaten first.
- Label all items with purchase/expiration dates.

- Group by category: grains, proteins, fruits, fats, condiments.

☞ **Checklist:**

✓ Label and organize all shelves

✓ Track expiration dates

✓ Plan weekly meals using stockpile

DAY 14: RUN A "NO STORE WEEK" TEST

- For 7 days, eat only from your pantry and water storage.
- Note challenges: Did you run out of variety? Struggle with cooking? Forget spices?
- Adjust stockpile based on real experience.

☞ **Checklist:**

✓ Complete 7-day pantry challenge

✓ Write down missing items

✓ Update shopping/stock list

END OF WEEK 2: YOUR FOOD & WATER LIFELINE

By now, you should have:

- A 30-day pantry with calorie-dense staples.
- A 3-day "grab-and-go" food reserve.
- At least 14 gallons of stored water per person.
- Two backup purification methods.
- An organized, rotating system that avoids waste.
- Confidence from your "no store" drill.

. . .

Food and water are the core of survival. With them secured, you're ready to move into **Week 3: Strengthen Your Home Base** — where we'll turn your house into a safe, resilient stronghold.

32 / WEEK 3: POWER & COMMUNICATIONS

FOOD AND WATER keep you alive. But in a collapse, **power and information** determine whether you stay safe, connected, and one step ahead. Blackouts make nights dangerous, cut off refrigeration, and silence news. Dead cell towers isolate families.

This week is about building a **layered backup system** for both electricity and communication, so that even when the grid goes down and phones stop working, you're never left in the dark.

DAY 15: LIGHT IN THE DARK

- Stockpile reliable lighting:
  - LED flashlights (with spare batteries).
  - Solar garden lights (charge during the day, bring inside at night).
  - Headlamps for hands-free use.
  - Candles as a last resort.
- Store at least **2 light sources per family member**.
- **Checklist:**

- ✓ Buy/organize LED flashlights & headlamps
- ✓ Store backup batteries
- ✓ Add solar or crank-powered lights

DAY 16: BACKUP POWER BASICS

- Get at least one **portable power bank** per person (for phones, radios).

- Add a **solar charger** or panel for recharging small devices.

- Consider a **portable generator** (gas, propane, or dual-fuel) for refrigerators or critical medical equipment.

Checklist:

- ✓ Power banks fully charged
- ✓ Solar panel or charger on hand
- ✓ Generator tested & fueled

DAY 17: ORGANIZE FUEL & FIRE

- Store extra propane, butane, or firewood safely.

- Practice using a **camp stove, rocket stove, or grill** for cooking.

- Rotate fuel stock regularly to avoid spoilage.

Checklist:

- ✓ At least one non-electric cooking method ready
- ✓ Fuel storage rotated and labeled
- ✓ Family trained in safe use

DAY 18: SECURE YOUR RADIOS

When phones die, radios take over.

- **NOAA Weather Radio:** For emergency alerts.
- **FRS/GMRS Walkie-Talkies:** Family/local communication.
- **Ham Radio (Optional):** Long-distance resilience if licensed.

☞ **Checklist:**

✓ NOAA weather radio tested

✓ FRS radios for family use

✓ Consider GMRS/ham for range

DAY 19: CREATE A FAMILY COMMUNICATION PLAN

- Choose a **primary contact method** (radio channel, signal).
- Set **check-in times** (morning/evening).
- Establish **meeting points** if separated.
- Write it down and keep a copy in every go-bag.

☞ **Checklist:**

✓ Family comms plan written

✓ Everyone knows channels/codes

✓ Meeting points agreed

DAY 20: TEST A BLACKOUT DRILL

- Shut off main power for 12–24 hours.
- Use only your backup systems.

- Note weaknesses: Did you run out of light? Could you cook? Stay in touch?

Checklist:

✓ Run blackout test

✓ Write down what failed

✓ Adjust supplies accordingly

DAY 21: BUILD A LAYERED SYSTEM

By the end of this week, you should have:

- **Light sources** (flashlights, headlamps, solar).
- **Backup power** (banks, solar, generator).
- **Cooking fuel & stoves.**
- **Radios & comms plan.**
- **Blackout-tested confidence.**

END OF WEEK 3: ALWAYS CONNECTED, NEVER POWERLESS

Now, even if the grid fails and cell towers collapse, your family will still have light, energy, and a way to stay informed and connected. That makes you safer, calmer, and more resilient than 90% of people in a blackout.

Next, in **Week 4: Build Long-Term Resilience**, we'll expand beyond short-term survival into sustainable systems — gardens, renewable energy, and the routines that let you thrive even if the crisis lasts for years.

33 / WEEK 4: TEST, DRILL, IMPROVE

By now, you've built a solid foundation: secured finances, stocked food and water, established backup power, and created a communication plan. But **supplies alone don't guarantee survival.** The key is practice. When a real emergency hits, hesitation, confusion, or missing steps can cost precious time.

This week is about **turning your plans into action** through drills, tests, and improvements. By practicing now, you build muscle memory and confidence — so when the collapse accelerates, your family acts with speed and calm instead of panic.

DAY 22: EVACUATION DRILL

- Pack go-bags and load the car in **under 10 minutes.**
- Drive your primary and secondary evacuation routes.
- Identify choke points, safe zones, and fuel stops.

Checklist:

✓ Family go-bags ready

✓ Car kit stocked and fueled

✓ Routes tested and adjusted

DAY 23: SHELTER-IN-PLACE DRILL

- Simulate a lockdown (storm, civil unrest, or curfew).

- Stay home 24 hours using only stored food, water, and power backups.

- Test lighting, cooking, security, and morale.

☞ **Checklist:**

✓ All family members involved

✓ Meals from pantry only

✓ Weak spots written down

DAY 24: COMMUNICATIONS DRILL

- Turn off phones and practice radio communication.

- Test NOAA alerts, FRS/GMRS walkie-talkies, and ham (if licensed).

- Stick to pre-set times and codes.

☞ **Checklist:**

✓ Radios tested

✓ Family knows how to use them

✓ Communication plan validated

DAY 25: SECURITY CHECK

- Walk your property at night.

- Test locks, lights, and alarms.

- Practice "quiet entry" drills with family (moving silently, dark navigation).

☞ Checklist:

✔ Exterior secured

✔ Night lighting functional

✔ Security drills practiced

DAY 26: BARTER SIMULATION

- Trade with a friend, neighbor, or family member.
- Use food, fuel, or small comfort items as barter.
- Practice negotiating fairly without revealing your full stockpile.

☞ Checklist:

✔ Barter items prepared

✔ Practice small exchanges

✔ Lessons written down

DAY 27: BLACKOUT CHALLENGE

- Shut off main breaker for **24 hours**.
- Live fully without grid power.
- Cook, light, and communicate using only backups.

☞ Checklist:

✔ 24 hours off-grid complete

✔ Weaknesses recorded

✔ Improvements planned

DAY 28: FAMILY REVIEW MEETING

- Gather the family.
- Ask: *What worked? What didn't? What do we need more of?*
- Update checklists and stockpile lists.

Checklist:

✓ Family feedback collected

✓ Action items listed

✓ Next steps assigned

DAY 29: IMPROVE & RESTOCK

- Fix weak points discovered during drills.
- Restock any food, fuel, or batteries used.
- Upgrade equipment if needed.

Checklist:

✓ Pantry & supplies replenished

✓ Gear repaired or replaced

✓ Systems refined

DAY 30: CONFIDENCE CHECK

- Review your journey: finances, food, water, power, comms, drills.
- Celebrate progress with your family.
- Commit to monthly mini-drills to keep sharp.

Checklist:

✓ Review progress

- ✓ Celebrate milestones
- ✓ Schedule ongoing practice

END OF WEEK 4: PREPARED, TESTED, AND READY

At the end of 30 days, you've gone from vulnerable to resilient. You've not only built supplies and systems, but you've **tested them, drilled them, and improved them.** You now hold the confidence that if the dollar collapses, your family won't just react — you'll respond with calm, clarity, and strength.

Preparedness isn't a one-time project. It's a way of life. Keep practicing, keep improving, and you'll stay ready for whatever comes.

CONCLUSION: FROM FEAR TO FREEDOM

You've just completed a journey that few people ever take. You've learned how fragile the dollar really is, how quickly systems can fail, and — most importantly — how to protect your family when they do.

At the beginning, maybe you felt fear. Fear of collapse. Fear of scarcity. Fear of not knowing what tomorrow holds. But now, after securing your finances, stockpiling food and water, preparing your home, practicing drills, and building inner strength, you hold something far greater than fear: **freedom.**

Preparedness isn't about living in constant worry. It's about living with confidence. You now know that if banks close, if stores empty, if lights go out, your family will still eat, drink, stay warm, and stay safe. You've tested your systems, found your weaknesses, and turned them into strengths. You've transformed uncertainty into stability.

Remember: survival is not just about supplies. It's about mindset, purpose, and community. It's about raising resilient children, helping neighbors, and passing on knowledge. It's about creating not just a way to endure collapse, but a way to thrive in the new world that follows it.

So don't stop here. Keep practicing. Keep drilling. Keep refining. Preparedness is not a 30-day sprint — it's a lifelong journey. The more you invest in resilience, the more freedom you gain from fragile systems.

One day, when others panic at empty shelves or silent ATMs, you'll feel calm. You'll know you've already done the work. And you'll look at your family and think: *We're ready. We'll endure. We'll overcome.*

This isn't the end of your preparedness journey. It's the beginning of a stronger, freer life. The collapse may come — but you will stand.

BONUS— READY-TO-USE TOOLS

All additional materials, including checklists, charts, and daily plans, are downloadable and printable through the QR code below

ACKNOWLEDGMENTS

This book would not have been possible without the support, encouragement, and contributions of many people.

First, I want to thank my family — for their patience during late nights of writing, for their belief in this mission, and for being my daily reminder of why this work matters.

To the friends, neighbors, and prepping community who shared ideas, tested drills, and gave honest feedback: your real-world insights strengthened every chapter.

A special thanks to [Editor Name], whose eagle eyes and wise suggestions helped sharpen the message. Also to [Designer Name] for envisioning a cover that captures urgency and hope in a single image.

Thank you to the survivors, historians, and veterans whose stories provided lessons and warnings — your voices live in these pages.

Finally, to you, the reader: by choosing to prepare instead of panic, you honor all who came before us and protect all who come after. May this book serve you well.

ABOUT THE AUTHOR

Don Clark Jr.

Survival strategist, author, and preparedness instructor

Don Clark Jr. has spent years researching economic collapse, readiness strategy, and community resilience. His work focuses on bridging practical survival skills with financial sense — a rare combination in preparedness literature.

As a writer and teacher, Don has delivered workshops across the U.S., conducted drills in remote terrain, and coached families in securing their homes, supplies, and minds. He believes resilience is not born of fear, but built through discipline, knowledge, and community.

Don lives in Texas with his family. When not writing or training, he maintains a home garden, experiments with renewable systems, and refines his emergency plans — always ready for the next challenge.

www.ingramcontent.com/pod-product-compliance
Lightning Source LLC
Chambersburg PA
CBHW032050150426
43194CB00006B/475